Making Policy Not Tea

Making Policy Not Tea
Women in Parliament

edited by
Arthur Baysting, Dyan Campbell,
and Margaret Dagg

Auckland
OXFORD UNIVERSITY PRESS
Melbourne Oxford   New York

Oxford University Press, Walton Street, Oxford OX2 6DP
Oxford   New York   Toronto
Delhi   Bombay   Calcutta   Madras   Karachi
Kuala Lumpur   Singapore   Hong Kong   Tokyo
Nairobi   Dar es Salaam   Cape Town
Melbourne   Auckland   Madrid
and associated companies in
Berlin   Ibadan

Oxford is a trade mark of Oxford University Press

Introduction, selection, and appendices © the editors 1993

This edition first published 1993

ISBN 19558275 6

Cover designed by Nikolas Andrew
Typeset in Times by Egan-Reid Ltd
Printed in New Zealand at GP Print Ltd
Published by Oxford University Press
1A Matai Road, Greenlane
PO Box 11-149, Auckland, New Zealand

CONTENTS

Acknowledgements

The editors would like to thank the MPs, who gave so freely their time and their ideas. We also acknowledge with gratitude the assistance of Members' parliamentary and electorate staff who were instrumental in arranging interviews and obtaining photographs. Thanks, too, are due to Kate Stone, Murray Beasley, and Anne French of Oxford University Press for their assistance; to Infofind Radio New Zealand for access to research material; to the Wellington Public and Auckland Public Library; to Ruth Dyson and Sue Wood; and to David Gee for material on Elizabeth McCombs from his forthcoming biography. Special thanks are particularly due to our partners, families, and friends for their patience.

The editors and publishers wish to express their gratitude to those MPs who made available photographs from their personal collections; and we wish to thank the following for permission to use illustrations: *The Christchurch Star*; *The Press*, Christchurch; *The New Zealand Herald*; South Pacific News Ltd, Wellington; *The Waikato Times*; Photography by Woolf Ltd, Wellington; Jocelyn Carlin; *The Evening Post*; Ernie Gilgen; Auckland Institute and Museum; Auckland Public Library; Waikato Museum of Art and History; *The Taupo Times*; Taupo Women's Club; H. B. Williams Memorial Library, Gisborne.

INTRODUCTION

Today's women Members of Parliament do not have an easy life. In addition to their parliamentary workload, their electorate duties, and the demands of their families, they feel a wider responsibility.

Just as New Zealand's first woman MP, Elizabeth McCombs, came to regard her constituency as transcending electoral boundaries and embracing women and women's interests throughout the country, so, today, there is a perception that women remain underrepresented in Parliament and that this imposes special responsibilities upon those of their number who are elected to political office. Even if they do not all consider themselves feminists, most women MPs admit to recognizing 'a thread that binds [them]'.

This book provides biographical details of the thirty-six women elected to the New Zealand House of Representatives, and a Parliament-by-Parliament analysis of the levels of women's representation since the 1930s. Photographs of the women MPs are also included. The main text, however, is drawn from interviews with women MPs, past and present. This provides a sharp contrast to usual practice.

When MPs are quoted in the news media they are generally speaking about Government or party policy. Their comments are usually abbreviated into the standard currency of short statements sandwiched between a reporter's introduction and a commentator's analysis. Before going out, the material is likely to have been shaped by a team of reporters, editors, and producers. MPs may have their own team shaping their material and polishing their performance before it is communicated via the media. There is nothing sinister in this. Media exposure is precious, and ten seconds on television or a five-line quote in a newspaper can be significant.

In compiling *Making Policy Not Tea* we have adopted, as far as possible, the opposite approach—one which encourages and appreciates spontaneity. We have researched existing material, but have interviewed only current and former women MPs. In each case the MP was interviewed only once. The alternative would have been to have revisited material and to have risked making changes that could have robbed the interviews of their freshness and compromised our original intention in embarking upon this project: to find out what MPs really think.

The interview material has been divided into chapters according to general themes. This is, in itself, a subjective exercise, but one which provides a collective insight that may not otherwise be so apparent. As the material was being compiled, common threads began to emerge. Nonetheless, the groupings are tentative, and there is considerable thematic cross-over and counterpoint between sections. The MPs have strong views on the way Parliament is run and how it might be improved. They discuss their private lives, explain their individual philosophies, and offer considered advice to anyone thinking of following in their footsteps. They give new perspectives on the Muldoon years and on the political turbulence of the Lange–Douglas era. Together, these common themes combine to create a fascinating overview of women's experience in Parliament. An examination of a traditionally male political institution cannot help but also be about men, and several women reminded us that life is also difficult for their male colleagues.

Most of the interviews were conducted in person; some were by telephone. In each case they were recorded by tape recorder and then transcribed and edited. MPs were given the opportunity to check their material. Of those who were given transcripts, none asked for any substantial changes.

Elizabeth Tennet, MP for Island Bay, 1987—, in Parliament, February 1993.

Initially, a few MPs declined to be interviewed and some perseverance was needed before permission was granted; but, once the interviews began, many seemed to relish the chance to talk. In every case, they happily went beyond the agreed time, although a couple of sessions were interrupted by the ubiquitous division bells. Almost all of the MPs revealed a strong sense of humour—a trait not always obvious on the page and certainly not often evident in their television soundbites.

In her retirement speech to the House, MP Fran Wilde described politics as 'the stuff of heart attacks and heartache'. Significantly, though, she added that she felt 'privileged to have been an MP'. This is a view shared by many of the women interviewed here. They have given us a picture of New Zealand politics previously unavailable, and we thank them for their honesty and their trust. We hope that we have produced a different kind of book from the existing analyses and surveys of New Zealand's political culture.

Elizabeth Reid McCombs
1873–1935

I'm not even tired.

Elizabeth McCombs was the first woman in New Zealand to be elected to Parliament. She died after being in the House for less than two years.

Politics was her life. With her two sisters, Christina and Stella Henderson, she was at the forefront of the women's movement of the time. She strongly supported her husband James's career, both before and after his election as Labour MP for Lyttelton. He dreamed of them being in the House together, and they stood for separate seats. In the event, Elizabeth's bids (in Kaiapoi, 1928, and Christchurch North, 1931) failed.

Elizabeth had a delicate constitution and suffered regular migraine and asthma attacks as a child. She was a vegetarian, and often so busy that she skipped mealtimes altogether. Photographs show her to have been extremely frail, and even she cheerfully described her health as 'wretched'.

In 1933, when James died of a heart attack, Elizabeth won the by-election. She began commuting to Wellington by inter-island ferry, leaving every Monday and returning every Friday.

Her role as the first woman MP was almost impossible to fill. She told friends that she was reluctant to open her mouth at meetings outside her electorate because, every time she did so, it led to dozens more invitations to speak. She received mountains of mail from women all over the country and answered every letter.

Following the birth of her son Terence—a future Minister of Education—in 1905 she spent long periods in bed; and, later, when she was campaigning she often rested in the day to gain strength to attend evening meetings.

To her colleagues, her death was not unexpected. One wrote that her health could not match her 'high ideal of Parliamentary service'. Elizabeth was a tee-totaller and, while her death certificate cited cirrhosis of the liver, the more likely cause of death was overwork and malnourishment.

She herself, however, was not ready to go: on her deathbed she said, 'I'm not done; I'm not even tired.'

Elizabeth Henderson (centre) with her sister, Christina, and her future husband, James McCombs, early 1900s. In 1933 Elizabeth McCombs became the first woman to be elected to the New Zealand House of Representatives.
Christchurch Star

Mary Batchelor, MP for Avon, 1972–87.
Christchurch Star

Colleen Dewe, MP for Lyttelton, 1975–78. Christchurch Star

1

STARTING OUT

The first women MPs tended to enter the House through direct family connections, often winning a seat vacated by a father or husband.

From the seventies onward there is no longer any such recognizable thread. Some MPs experienced a political awakening at secondary school or university; others entered the political arena by way of the unions or local government; and others again had their first experience of politics through Plunket or playcentre. Issues such as the Vietnam War, nuclear-free, and the Springbok tour also played their part.

Marilyn Waring

. . . it's extraordinarily lonely.

When I first went in, there were four of us in there. Colleen Dewe was elected for Lyttelton. There was Whetu Tirikatene-Sullivan and Mary Batchelor.

It was extraordinary. I had been a research officer in Parliament so I thought I had a fair idea of what I was letting myself in for. But no matter what familiarity you have with day-to-day activities, nothing prepares you for Government Caucus—just nothing in your life. Particularly if you happen to be a twenty-three-year-old feminist. And it's extraordinarily lonely.

There's no doubt that, particularly, the entry of Colleen Dewe and myself was assisted by the fact that we followed immediately on International Women's Year and so there had been a lot of activity. There was a highly energized, highly mobile, highly participatory women's movement, particularly in terms of submissions to select committees, lobbying Members of Parliament and so on.

That energy sustained itself, I would say, through the abortion debates— there were two or three of them in that parliamentary period. Then, to a certain extent, that energy level receded throughout the rest of my term in Parliament.

It was affected by the fact that we were all participating in the anti-apartheid movement, we were all participating in the nuclear-free movement. Some of the material legislative reforms that upper-class and middle-class women would have wanted, for example in equal pay and matrimonial property legislative reform, had been achieved. A number of the access questions, whether it was access to juries, women JPs and so on, were either being passed or given token acknowledgement.

Whetu Tirikatene-Sullivan

The Treaty of Waitangi . . . was the pivot of all justice
and the axis of our dignity . . . I am here in Parliament
as a Māori advocate.

I was born and reared in Rātana Pā. The man whom I personally consider to have been one of the greatest Māori leaders, Tahupotiki Wiremu Rātana, named me. He had been the subject of Māori prophesy, as the leader who would emerge with the Treaty of Waitangi in one hand and the Bible in the other. Those who followed him pledged adherence to both. Thus was the powerful Rātana movement brought into existence. He personally arranged for us children to be reared in this dual philosophy.

My parents had literally given up a flourishing business and farm in the South Island to follow Rātana, living on their own savings for twelve years, in order to join Rātana in his mission. They were years of hardship but the poverty was perceived to be a privilege by my devout parents. I remember those days with nostalgia. The Rātana Marae was a place of prayer and political debate; the Treaty of Waitangi was familiar to me as a very young child. It was the pivot of all justice and the axis of our dignity.

My father was Rātana's political advisor, upholding the rights and responsibility of the Māori according to the third article of that Treaty. That was the crucible in which I was moulded. From that, I continue to insist that there must be a guarantee of Māori advocacy in the New Zealand House of Representatives.

Before the Treaty of Waitangi was 'popular' it was integral to me. Equally central and seminal in my life were the scriptures. Rātana evangelized in both areas. Those who followed him were given the name, 'Morehu' (from the scriptural term, 'the remnants'). We became a supra-tribal Māori people, and numbered 40,000.

In 1932, as the first of Rātana's candidates to enter Parliament, my father presented the Rātana petition seeking statutory recognition of the Treaty of Waitangi. It was signed by the majority of Māori adults. So, I come not as a stranger to this subject.

I am here in Parliament as a Māori advocate. My advocacy is on behalf of all the Māori people, irrespective of tribe. I have drafted more private member's bills than I have introduced, all deriving from my Rātana origins. One was the Treaty of Waitangi Reconciliation Bill; another was my Māori Representation Amendment Bill. Others which got further were the Māori Language Bills.

The Māori Language Bill came twenty years after my first action as a student leader, as Vice-President of the Victoria University Students' Federation and founding President of the New Zealand Māori Students' Federation. There was no good reason why Māori should not be offered along with several other languages in our universities, but it took twenty-five years of continual effort before it was offered at all New Zealand universities. I kept up my interest throughout that period. Now, it is taken for granted.

Sonja Davies

I had ninety-six street-corner meetings. . . .

The first time I stood for selection was in 1966 in Rotorua, and I was the first one up. I was petrified, I had no idea. For me it was a new experience. I knew no one in Rotorua; I stayed at a hotel and I was just left alone. No one wants to know you just before the selection. No one wants to have anything to do with you and it's very, very lonely.

Then there was terrible weather, the planes weren't flying, the Head Office selection people had to drive up, and they were very late. When they got there they said we're going to cut [the selection speech] down to five minutes. I wasn't skilled at that time. I'd done a special one for fifteen minutes and it was hard for me to quickly know what I needed to jettison, and there were a lot of us in for that seat. And so I didn't get that.

So then I went on to Taupō and stood for that one, and Stan Rodger was in for selection. There was another guy who had been in Rotorua who had a small child with him, and he gave [the child] to me to look after while he went and practised his speech in the toilet.

I didn't get that, and I know I could have won the seat in Taupō. My parents were National Party, and they knew I would have won Taupō. Norman Kirk didn't help me at all and when I tackled him later he said, 'Well, you're on the national executive. It wouldn't look good if I seem to favour you.'

From Taupō I went to Hastings and I got that. But I thought that Hastings was sort of like another Nelson and it wasn't. It was much more brash and everybody had two or three jobs. Watties was booming and people got up early and picked asparagus and strawberries or whatever. Then they went and did their job. And at night they went on the assembly line. I did it on an anti-Vietnam platform, and Havelock North and other places are full of retired colonels, and various people didn't like that at all. I can remember talking about how we needed to increase the level of our overseas aid, and them saying, 'To hell with that, what we want to know is, what would Labour do about secondary taxation?'

I had ninety-six street-corner meetings, and they'd never had them before. So that was quite fun. Then I got beaten up at one—some guy took to me. I was talking about housing actually. I've never known why he did it. The police rang me up and said, 'Have you got any bruises? Did he break anything?' And they were very disappointed when I said I was just sore where he hit me. He had a grudge about something.

My opponent, Duncan MacIntyre, was in his element. He'd been in there and was about to become a Cabinet minister. He was a real politician. He could go along and talk abstinence and temperance to the Temperance League and go to the RSA and have a beer with the boys and be accepted by both. But it was a good experience.

The next time I stood was in Nelson in '78 when Stan Whitehead died. I stood in the selection for Nelson with Geoffrey Palmer, Stan Rodger, Malcolm McNamara, and a guy called Mel Courtney. I'd been away for eight years. I'll never forget that night. My son Mark came over from Rai Valley and sat there with his bush shirt on. He said, 'You're bloody mad doing it again. They won't have you.'

Bill Rowling was there, and Rai Valley was in his electorate. I introduced him to Mark and he said, 'You're a constituent of mine.' Mark said, 'I wouldn't bank on it, Mr Rowling, I'm a socialist.' Bill said, 'Just like your bloody mother.' So that was Nelson. I thought, 'That's it. They don't want me.' It really hurt me. Later on Philip Woollaston used to say to me, 'You should have been the Member' and 'you still should be the Member and you'd just be retiring now.'

I went to a couple of international women's conferences. I went to the United Nations conference on women in Mexico in 1975. There was an incident in the plenary session. There were a lot of male games being played, most of the women's delegations had male diplomats who sat behind them telling them what to say. There were big arguments about Zionism and the Palestinians.

And Whetu Tirikatene-Sullivan was there and she was so angry she seized the microphone and talked about what the conference was really about. She got huge applause. And Mary Sinclair spoke out in the committee. The thing that really horrified us was the way that women were manipulated by the male diplomats. We had a woman diplomat, Priscilla Williams, who is the High Commissioner to India at the moment. She was wonderful.

Then we went to Nairobi in 1985. For a lot of women that changed their lives quite dramatically. It was at that conference that I began to feel very unhappy at being pushed into the Western group. Every morning they'd meet and discuss the conference and what was likely to happen, and so on. And I just felt, I don't belong here. I'd rather be with the non-aligned people because that's where all the indigenous people are. There was this growing awareness that we weren't part of the British Empire on which the sun never set, we were a nation—a Pacific country, and therefore that's who we should be talking to. Of course that wasn't a popular idea.

The women's conventions were never well-reported. The media were new to it too. There was a big argument about whether there should be any male reporters. A lot of energy was taken up with those sorts of things.

I don't think it would have been possible, with hindsight, but it would have been good if we could have got alongside the guys and said, 'Now, you set up your own organization for talking to each other because life's not all a bowl of cherries for you either. You've been brought up not to cry, you've been brought up not to be emotional, you've been brought up to have stiff upper lips and that's done things to you. It makes it hard for you to be a warm, caring, loving spouse and father. It's not your fault, but you've got to work that through yourselves.' They're starting to do that now, with each other.

Helen Clark

The male MPs were used to women playing a
subordinate and service role in their lives.

Dad was not a Labour supporter. He was chair of the Te Pahu branch of the National Party and very supportive of Marilyn Waring. He probably would have loved me to have been the National MP for the area, but it couldn't be. He then sort of transferred all the energy into supporting her. He liked Marilyn and when the pressures came on against her and all the rumours and the whispers about her sexuality, my parents were never party to that at all.

When I went in we had forty MPs and the new MPs in the first fifteen to sixteen months had no specific responsibilities at all. Everyone who'd been there before had something. It was still in the days when you tended to have a shadow ministry and that sort of thing. An Opposition backbencher's life is not a great one; it's not terribly fulfilling. Funnily enough I think with only twenty-nine MPs in the [Labour] Caucus, like at present, they can play a more useful role. With so few people, they end up getting jobs.

At first it was very hard. Six women MPs wasn't enough. Fran Wilde and Margaret Shields and myself were treated pretty badly in many respects. There was some really entrenched dislike of women. You were dealing with old-style Labour men who just didn't see you. The whole tone of the place was appalling. It was almost indescribable how awful it was. In those days most politicians' wives would not have been in any sort of paid work. The male MPs were used to women playing a subordinate and service role in their lives.

We'd been doing a lot of work to get more women candidates and increase participation. It was just a question of that working it's way through the system. When I ran for the nomination here in 1980 there were still people who went around saying women would lose votes and lose the seat and that sort of thing. But even by '84 I think they had gone. And Fran and Margaret Shields won marginal seats. So people started to see that women might actually be an advantage, not a disadvantage.

Katherine O'Regan

I don't think he found it very easy to take, to be beaten by a woman. He was a nice chap, but that's what happens in politics.

I guess I grew up with political life. My father was always interested in politics, consequently so was my mother, but my father was the one who was involved. So there was always political activity. Not radical stuff. We were hill-country farmers and fairly conservative as you can imagine.

My grandmother influenced me a lot more than I realized in that she believed very strongly in looking after family or whānau. She hated the State intervening at any stage. She loathed and detested the Department of Labour, which in those days used to come round and check your business, because Grandpa had a trucking business. She refused to accept the old age pension, and when she was about seventy-five Mum dragged her into the Social Security Department and said, 'Come on, you're entitled to it—you should have it.' But Nana believed in looking after herself. The State was for somebody else, it wasn't for her. In a way that probably fits my philosophy.

In those days the men always became involved in the political world—it wasn't the women so much. Not in my world anyway. And my father was chairman of the local branch, and I think my mother may have been the secretary for a while. One regret is my father died before I went into politics. Even before I became a county councillor. And that saddened me, because he had been a county councillor and I would have loved to have been able to share things too. Unfortunately I couldn't because he'd gone.

Mum still keeps a very active interest in politics. She never tried to stop me, but at first she was a bit horrified that her daughter would consider doing these things. But I think she was very proud that I had. My first political involvement, if you can call it political, was becoming involved with Plunket. I missed all the teenage things. I never joined Young Nats. I didn't become involved in any political action, be it Vietnam or any of those things. I seemed to watch from the outside, but I never felt a part of that. Many of my contemporaries would have been in the thick of anti-Vietnam marches and that sort of thing. But I wasn't.

I was one of those sort of people: you want to see things change so you go along to an annual general meeting. You get up and say, 'Look, why aren't you doing x, y, z?' They say, 'Oh, that's a good idea.' Then you get on to the election of officers. And it's 'what about you being the secretary or vice-something-or-other?'

It happened like that with Plunket. I decided, like my mother and my grandmother, to become involved in Plunket. I was out in the country, but I helped a central city branch. I initiated some fundraising, doing catering for clearing sales. Us young mothers would hurl up in the van. My first husband owned a sawmill, and we used the van to cart all the trestles and pie-warmers and pick up the pies and the bread and the corned beef for the sandwiches, and grated cheese and pineapple; and we'd hurl off to some farm in June when it was freezing cold, set everything up in the cowshed, and make sandwiches. But I seemed to find myself in some of the top positions as soon as I arrived at something. I didn't mind because I felt that I had something to offer and that if I could help—that was really the motivation.

I was only at primary school when Dad was on the council. I quite enjoyed looking at the maps and listening to Dad talk about the roads. And I must admit I did enjoy playing with toy trucks and digging roads in the garden with my brothers.

When it came to the local body elections in, I think, 1977, I decided I'd give it a go with Waipa Council. My husband at the time was having a row with the council, and he reckoned I could do the job just as well. He and a group of others said, 'Why don't you give it a go? There's never been a woman councillor. See if you can unseat the person who's there and get on to the council and try and fix these things up.'

So I did; I stood and I beat the man. I don't think he found it very easy to take, to be beaten by a woman. He was a nice chap, but that's what happens in politics. I held on to that riding until I retired in 1984 to go into Parliament. At the time of the council election I said I'd knock on every door and I think I did. In those days campaigning as such was not heard of. I'd developed a calling card with my photograph on it and a little bit of background—what my key views were on where I thought the council should go. I left that on the doorstep for people if they weren't home.

It was the first time I think it had ever been done—certainly in Waipa. I was really only copying what I'd learnt from the 1975 campaign when I worked for Marilyn Waring and the National Party. I just used those same skills and applied them to local government.

Marie Hasler

'For heaven's sake, stop talking about it and do something.' So I did.

My parents were National. They were business people but not active politically. I don't know where I got my interest in politics, to be quite honest. It might have been at school. I think it's just something you're interested in or not.

Some people think you're crazy; politics bores the pants off them. Others are vitally interested, and I've always been one of them. Politics is so much a part of life. I was always interested in how society works, who was standing, how their campaign would go, who was going to beat whom. I find it quite exciting.

I was first active about twenty years ago when I helped someone who stood for a seat in this area. I've always been a political animal. I did have the dream, if that isn't being too melodramatic, of one day being the MP for Titirangi. But it had always been a Labour seat, so it wasn't a very realistic proposition. And I was doing other things; I had interesting jobs and I had my own business.

So it was always in the back of my mind, but because I was so busy I didn't give it the attention I should have. Then after I'd sold my business I became a manager, and my partner kept saying, 'For heaven's sake, stop talking about it and do something.' So I did.

Anne Collins

I'd never even seen Parliament sit . . .

I was a teacher at high school. I was a Labour Party branch secretary. When

I decided to stand I thought I had absolutely no chance of winning. Then about a month out I got a fright when I realized it was a definite possibility. And that did shock me. I think I stopped eating for about the last three weeks of the campaign, I was so nervous about it all.

The selection was, 'Would you please do it?' I said, 'Yes, I suppose so, I don't want to go back teaching full-time until next year.' The LEC thought they'd like a woman candidate, and there was nobody interested. Forty-three years of National-held seat; it would have had to have been someone who just wanted to practise. Basically they just asked me if I'd do it.

Anne Hercus and Margaret Shields were the ones who encouraged me to think about sitting in the first place. So they were here. And Helen Clark was in. And Whetu, she was lovely. Fran Wilde was really supportive. Margaret Austin came in with us. The Labour Women's Caucus met every week; we had lunch together every Thursday.

When I became an MP I didn't know what to expect. I'd never even seen Parliament sit so in a way it was culture shock. Annette King and Judy Keall came in with me. They were my buddies.

Christine Fletcher

'Oh, Chrissie dear, who's going to take care of your family?'

For me, politics really came about because of a frustration that women—particularly women with a background in small business in New Zealand—weren't being adequately represented.

I come from a traditional National Party background. My mother came from a farming background, my father was a manufacturer, so they were the traditonal core support if you look back in terms of conservative politics in New Zealand—manufacturers' lobby and the farmers' lobby.

My grandmother, my mother's mother, had come from Canterbury to be in Auckland as a support person for my mother. She was, I suppose, an early feminist, and she had not really done particularly well within her own family unit. The farm had been left to her brothers. She got married and they had a big mortgage and they went through the Depression and those sorts of things. But she was a very articulate woman, very much a dominant force in my life. She was the person who enabled my mother to travel, helped my father grow the business, and all those sorts of things.

Papakura, which is where I was born and brought up, was tremendously important in that it was a mix of urban and rural and a mix of Māori and

Pākehā. I'm tremendously grateful for that. It gave me an awareness of issues that I might not have had, had I grown up in the heart of Remuera. No offence. Or had I grown up in the middle of wherever else.

I went to Papakura Central until I was eleven. For secondary schooling I was sent to St Cuthbert's College. I hated St Cuthbert's. I hated the travelling. I became somewhat rebellious, and I was packed off to board in the fourth form. I escaped that for the fifth and sixth form, but I was sent off again for the seventh form. I was a bit of a truant, and the headmistress at the time said to my mother, 'Either we can find alternative education for Christine elsewhere in the education system or maybe she'd like to board.' I did very well in terms of music and drama and areas where I could use my creativity, but I just found the arbitrary rules very suppressive. A lot of women probably share that but they enjoy the camaraderie of other women in single sex schools. It's not unlike Parliament for me now—just mindless rules. The divisions that just go on.

I've had this 'flu all week, and I kept getting packed off to talk to women's committees all around the countryside. My ears played up, and at about nine yesterday morning I'd had it. So I went to the Whips and said, 'I want to go home, I want to lie in my own bed and have a lemon drink.' And it was, 'No, you can't; we don't have enough people; we can't form a

Christine Fletcher, MP for Eden, with her sister, Sue Lees, and her mother, Shirley Lees, on election night, 1990.

quorum.' This went on all day until finally at about eight o'clock I said, 'I'm going. Sorry if you don't like it, you'll have to give me a detention, but I'm going.' It's just that sort of mindless stuff that got up my nose. A lot of the time at school I just couldn't see the purpose.

My father was resentful that he didn't have a son, and he wanted us to be independent. So when I was fifteen and my sister was eighteen, he gave us passports and packed us off round the Pacific by ourselves. He wanted for us to be able to handle ourselves. He was happy for me to have a car. I had an old Anglia van, and I travelled to and from school with that. I think secretly he liked me being a rebel and he didn't really get offended that I was a bit of a truant. My truancy was pretty harmless stuff, by comparison to today.

Before he taught me to swim we used to have boating holidays. My mother was appalled when he tied a rope around me and threw me overboard and said, 'Now keep kicking, keep kicking, you'll be fine.' I liked the challenge in it. Or maybe I grew to expect that.

Since then I've constantly put up challenges for myself. I've sought out situations where I test myself. I was the first woman to jump from this parachute club when I was sixteen or seventeen. I've always tested myself in different ways, particularly sporting challenges.

In terms of the issues that really motivated me to sacrifice my life—which I think you really do as a woman trying to balance your family life and politics—it was the community organizations that I became involved with. I was frustrated that they didn't have the representation that they needed. I'm still involved with some now—Substance Abuse Trust, organizations dealing with drug and alcohol abuse, the Red Cross, the advocacy of elderly people. As long as I can remember there was always something that we were passionate about that was right for our community. I believe in power at a local level and in communities empowering themselves.

My father also had very strong feelings about how the family business was run. We worked in the school holidays. You had to go learn to operate the PABX or the machinery of the time, whatever it might be. Even though we might be just six or seven, that was all part of my father's idea of training the girls. You never had any spare money because you put it back in the business, so you didn't have fancy cars or clothes. Father brought me up to almost despise overt affluence. I disliked the eighties intensely because of that, and I'm very grateful for that now, because things like that don't mean that much to me.

I stood firstly in Papakura. Selection came up there because Merv Wellington retired, and I only decided to put my name in the hat at the last minute. I knew most of the voting delegates, they had already committed their allegiance to John Robertson who was the candidate there. It was a very good training ground for me in terms of realizing that it's not enough to just be a good candidate, you also have to be a good strategist. You've got to be there to do the deals, sign them up—boys' club stuff.

When I went round to the delegates their first question inevitably was, 'Oh, Chrissie dear, who's going to take care of your family?' I played into their hands by being defensive and trying to rationally explain the support mechanisms that I would have in place. By the time I lost out—and I put up a good campaign—I was quite bitter. When I got their letters later on saying, 'Oh, we wish we'd voted for you', I didn't even bother to respond to them.

Then I went back to Eden which was where we'd lived for the last ten years. I would have liked Papakura because it was close to my family. I knew the issues out there probably better than I did in Eden. I would have the support of my mother, particularly. I mean, at that stage, Jen was three and Andrew was nine. It would be one whole lot easier.

In hindsight I'm happy that it's worked out the way that it has because Eden is an urban electorate and I'm definitely closer to the mood of what the people of Eden want. When the voting delegates asked me who was going to look after my kids I told them it was none of their business—why didn't they ask me about my administrative capabilities. I was much more arrogant and I really didn't care if I didn't get selected. But if I was going to be selected it was going to be on my own terms.

Jenny Kirk

'What do you do with your feminist politics?'

I was involved in personal politics for quite a while. By that I mean women's politics. In 1973 I returned to New Zealand and was very keen to go to the 1973 Auckland Women's Convention,

It came up out of the Women's Liberation movement which had developed in the late 1960s and early 1970s. There were international speakers. Over a period of time I had realized that there was more to life than just getting married and having kids. Which was what I had been brought up to expect. That was to be my lot in life, to live happily ever after.

It didn't quite seem totally satisfactory. It also didn't gel with my experiences as a married woman. I actually did have to have a job. I also needed child care, which was very difficult to find. So there were a whole lot of things. Those women were saying things that I had an empathy with and I thought, 'I can understand that, that sounds right to me.'

1975 was International Women's Year. By that time I was living in

Hastings and I was involved with the National Organisation for Women, just a little group, doing our bit for International Women's Year.

Among our members was a woman who was running her own business very successfully, but the power board wouldn't send her an account in her own name. She couldn't get the power on, or the telephone, without it going through her husband who had nothing at all to do with her business. So we used her as an example of inequality for women.

Then there was the abortion debate, and when I came back up to Auckland I became involved with that. We had to do a lot of organizing to get thousands of women's signatures on one petition. So those were things I personally believed in. It seemed to me that if the community had support groups for women and children and if society looked after their health and education and housing, then women had the basis for a family life that had some stability. Given these conditions, you would have people growing up who were productive citizens, who weren't a drain on the welfare system, ones who didn't end up with suburban neurosis because of depression and so on.

That was a developing theme that I had from those early years, and I still hold those beliefs. I still had to work to help the family finances. I had small children and I found that quite stressful because there wasn't much support in the community for it.

Happy ever after was not so happy, and eventually my marriage broke up and I became a solo parent. I continued to work, but after a year of full-time work and custodial responsibility for my children, my physical health deteriorated and I had no choice but to go on the DPB. While I was on it I found time to evaluate my own life: look at what I wanted to do.

I was living in Northcote, on the North Shore of Auckland. I had grown up in that area. With boundary changes, a new seat was put in and that was Glenfield. I had grown up in Glenfield.

I had long discussions with friends along the line of, 'What do you do with your feminist politics? Do you try and change things via mainstream politics, or do you try and change them from women's separatist politics?'

I was a mainstream person, so when the Glenfield seat came up I felt it was about time I actually started doing something with mainstream politics. So I joined the Labour Party and offered my writing skills to be their publicity person. I know Glenfield. I've lived in that area for a long time and that was also a useful asset.

As a result I did do a lot of publicity work for Glenfield, for the Labour Party. And the Labour Party was successful in winning that seat. Afterwards Judy Keall, who was the MP, said to me would I like to be her electorate secretary? I had done secretarial work, I had been a writer, and so I said yes.

I started and I realized after a while that I also had the skills that would suit a life in politics. Not public speaking, which I didn't have a skill in at all, but I figured I'd pick it up after a while.

It seemed to me that political life was about being in the forefront of changing things and for standing up for what you believed in. I wanted to see a better society where women and children were acknowledged and treated as important, and where they were given opportunities that were equal to those of men.

I thought I could do it for Birkenhead. It seemed there were a lot of people who believed like I did—who seemed to be liberal and feminist-minded and conservation-minded and so on. And they all lived in Birkenhead. Labour had minimal organization and I had gone through an election campaign in Glenfield so I had knowledge and organizing skills and started to organize for the Labour Party in Birkenhead.

I had helped Cath Tizard while I was on the DPB. I had helped Judy Keall. I had attended seminars dealing with local government politics and Labour politics and I thought I should give it a go. I gave it a go in Birkenhead, and I was selected. A week later Jim McLay resigned, which threw the seat wide open.

I went into Parliament because I had experience with the children, with the playcentre, and the need for crèches and hospitals and health and in the paid workforce. All of those things I thought related to everyday living.

I also understood that politicians made decisions that related to everyday living. So I did have a firm belief that I went in there with value, that I could say that these decisions you are making are going to impact on people.

Any women considering going into politics need to know themselves. They need to know they have the strength to believe in themselves. They have to have a philosophy to go in with. I don't care what that philosophy is, but they have to have a belief in their philosophy.

My philosophy was: how is this going to affect women and children? You have to have something to measure the policies against, and you have to have that very deeply and firmly inside you. If it's just something that you picked out of the air, then it's not something that you can hold on to, because politics does make you question your own beliefs.

It makes you question yourself, the way that the system is run and what goes on in there. You need to know how your party works, you need to have built up an understanding of how the party works, and perhaps have some experience of working within the party so you have credibility among some party people. If you have these beliefs then you can argue from a position of personal strength. If you don't have a personal philosophy then you can be manipulated by the political process.

Margaret Austin

*. . . the family was required to sit around the old radio
and listen to Walter Nash.*

My childhood memories of politics are of my parents not being able to talk
in any way at all about conservative policies. I have Budget night indelibly
imprinted on my memory where the family was required to sit around the
old radio to listen to Walter Nash. So in that sense I suppose you were
imbued with the fact that up here there was a centre of power which was the
Government. And election nights were just dreadful if Labour didn't win.
My parents were very traditional Labour.

My mother reminded me after the '84 election that I once said that one
day I'd be an MP, but I have no recollection of that myself. But I did
understand early that the only way to make changes was to be a politician
oneself. It has never seemed strange to me for a woman to go into anything
she chose to go into.

I came through a time in my childhood when the men were at war and the
women did everything. It's not part of your experience that the women were
not involved in the workforce, or not involved in doing things.

I became a member of the Labour Party at some stage during the 1972–
75 period. I was so incensed by the politicking of Sir Robert Muldoon during
the 1975 campaign, I was determined I was going to throw my oar in in an
active way to try and do something to stop that juggernaut.

In the event, I was only active at election time, and then had the
opportunity to go to England, to the Institute of Education as a Commonwealth Trust Fellow in 1980–81. I found at that time that the policies of the
Thatcher Government were becoming evident in their attempts to impose
an ideology on education.

The Institute was highly politicized. The topics of conversation centred
around what was happening in the political arena and particularly how they
were going to impact on educational management. It was at the time when
the Social Democrat Party broke away from the Labour Party and it seemed
to me that the SDP at that time was then much more in line with the New
Zealand Labour Party than the British Labour Party.

It was that combination of events which decided me: 'Right, when I get
home I'll become involved in a branch.' That's what I did. Then in 1982
Mick Connelly indicated that he was intending to retire. By that time I was
the branch chairperson and the delegate to the Labour Electorate Committee,
and we started to think about the likely candidates for the seat.

I then was on the receiving end of a representation by members and from people in other branches to see whether I would allow my name to go forward. And I was very actively involved in education. While attracted to the notion, it took a long time to make the commitment that, yes, I was prepared to change direction in my life because that's what it would mean, but I eventually sought the nomination and got it.

My first reaction was a mixture of flattery and apprehension. It's a whole new dimension and I had to sit back and think, 'Now, if you're going to seek the nomination it is inconceivable that you're not going to go out and set about to win it.' And you have to work out how it was you were going to do that. So it was like a mini-campaign.

There were ten people nominated for the candidacy, so there was quite a good degree of competition from within the electorate. It is exciting, because obviously once you had made your decision you were committed. Then, once you set out, you had to fulfil the commitment.

You got a taste of what it was like to go out canvassing. You had to canvass all the members to see whether they would be prepared to support you with the floor vote by turning up to the selection meeting. Then you had the speech to prepare. You've only got twelve minutes, and you'll be penalized for speaking over time: every word has to count.

And it was a very important election coming up to 1984. I had to meet with branch people and talk to them about my aspirations and the sort of way you would want to operate in the electorate, the sort of support you would give to people, the degree to which you were prepared to be available.

I was the deputy principal of a school, so organization was no problem to me at all. After the selection the first thing I did was go back to the LEC with an overall plan for the management of the campaign and the organization within the electorate. The sorts of groups that I thought ought to be part of the team and to whom they would report and what the financial arrangements would be and so on. So we got ourselves underway.

And we'd done an enormous amount of canvassing prior to the '84 election. We had a system of groups who had specific functions, and we had a campaign team made up of the co-ordinators. Then the snap election was announced about six months early and we were thrown into it. There was a very strong women's branch—mainly middle-aged to elderly women. But very, very supportive. They made sure there were willing co-ordinators.

Margaret Shields

*. . . through . . . trying to persuade women to make policy
not tea, in the end, I was persuaded to stand myself.*

I can't remember how or when it become obvious that I was going to end up
in politics. It certainly became obvious to other people a little earlier than it
did to me. But my interest in politics really arose out of my earlier interest in
women's issues.

I was married very young, went to live in a new house in a very new
suburb very early in our married life. I realized what had happened in postwar New Zealand wasn't exactly ideal for women. There seemed to be a
tremendous amount of isolation. The happily-ever-after bit that was
supposed to happen according to the magazines certainly didn't seem to be
flourishing in the area where we were living.

I got involved with forming the Society for Research on Women. We
started to do research on trying to find out what women wanted, what their
situation really was, and what could positively be done about it.

At that stage I had a somewhat naïve belief that if we demonstrated to
politicians what needed to be done they would simply spring to attention and
say 'goodness gracious!' and do it. Life isn't quite like that.

Mr Muldoon was a factor in my deciding to get involved in joining the
Labour Party. At that stage neither of my parents would have been Labour
voters. My father was very traditional and believed his daughters should get
a job and then get married.

There was a series of talks put on by the Linden Playcentre. I can
remember most of the lecturers. There was Doris McDonald, who was with
the Labour Department, and Miriam Gilson, who was a lecturer in sociology
at Victoria University. There was Dr Fraser McDonald and Bill Sutch—Dr
W. B. Sutch. Another was Beverly Morris, who was a specialist in early
childhood education.

It was an initiative from the playcentre, it was part of the normal
education programme, but there was something really special about those
lectures—they were actually based on the Voice of America series, *The
Potential of Women.*

Instead of the usual sort of dozen reluctant mums who are drummed up
to go to a parent education lecture or lecture series, this attracted 300 women
from all over Wellington. They came from as far away as Upper Hutt to go
to Linden. So we realized it was striking a chord for a whole lot of women.
I was twenty-three or twenty-four—a typical bored suburban housewife.

I got involved in politics to be involved in policy formation rather than to become a politician. But through being involved in the social policy and women's policy area of the Labour Party and travelling around New Zealand trying to persuade women to make policy not tea, in the end I was persuaded to stand myself.

I remember the 1972 elections because I was out doing my duty at the polling-booth and I arrived home just as the first results were starting to come through. It was very clear that it was a landslide and my mother clearly thought she had somehow or other caused it.

By the time I actually got into political life I had observed it at pretty close quarters for long enough to not be terribly surprised at anything. I was naïve to start with, but by the time I actually got in I knew what it was about. I delayed standing for a winnable seat until such time as my family was at a stage where it wasn't going to be too traumatic for them.

I started in Karori in 1975 because I knew I couldn't win it. It was great fun. I wanted to have the opportunity of standing in a seat where I could test myself out. I didn't know whether I could be a politician or not. If you stand in a seat which traditionally belongs to the other party you can be yourself in a way that you can't in a seat which is truly winnable. That means that you've got people breathing down your neck and if you make a mistake then somebody's going to say, 'I told you so'. It allows you a great deal more freedom.

I always believed that people prefer to be told the truth even if it isn't what they want to hear, rather than to have politicians trying to please everybody on all sides and sounding fudgy. That was certainly what happened in Karori because there were a number of fairly controversial debates going on at the time.

There was the so-called white paper on health, which I felt quite comfortable about going out and defending but most candidates were running scared from at the time. The issues were quite complicated, but once you started pulling the rhetoric away, explaining what happened, people sort of said, 'Yeah, yeah, no one ever explained that to me before.' There was the issue of trade unionism. There was an immigration debate going on. The most controversial debate of all that formed part of that election was the abortion debate.

And I felt it was necessary to make my position clear and I had a lot of people ringing me, quite desperate, wanting me to say, no, I wouldn't vote against the abortion, or I'd changed my mind or whatever, and I'd explain why I had my position and say, 'Look, if you can't support that I understand.' These were traditional Labour voters who were really torn. After the election people were coming up to me, sometimes several years later, saying, 'I voted for you even though—'because you explained why.

That was part of learning for me. And I also have always believed that if you compromise your views for expedient reasons on the way into politics, you're not much use to yourself, or anybody else probably, ever again. It's much more likely to happen if you haven't had the opportunity of standing where it doesn't matter.

In 1978 I won on the night and increased the vote after specials, and then lost on a technicality.[1] It was awful. In a sense, I ended up feeling worse for the people who worked for me than I did for myself.

I was definitely robbed. It wasn't a fair result and that was borne out later by the declaratory judgment brought out by a unanimous decision of five High Court judges. But the clause relating to the intention of voters takes precedence over the letter of instruction.

Unfortunately the first judgment was against us. It was not a unanimous judgment either. But at the time we'd already been through seven or eight months of trauma, and it was going to cost an enormous amount of money to carry on for an uncertain result. I wasn't going to put anybody through that any more.

It's sort of water under the bridge. One of the wise things that was said to me at the time has lived with me ever since. I had said, somewhat pathetically I guess, I only wanted justice. And someone said to me, 'You don't go to court for justice, you go for a judgment.'

Elizabeth Tennet

We were angry because we received feedback that we were just being hysterical females. That was a bit of a turning-point in understanding.

It started in my high school years. The age of fourteen was very formative for me, and I made a decision to become involved politically with a small 'p'. I didn't know how I would do that, but I certainly decided that's what I wanted.

Then I went to university and it was the period of the anti-war demonstrations, which I was very active in. I became involved in HART before the Springbok tour. I was at university from 1970 to 1973, so I was involved in all those international political issues. I joined the Labour Party when I was at university and I've been active ever since.

Dad was vaguely involved on the fringes of the Social Credit Party, but he came from a strong Labour background and there was a strong interest in international affairs. He was very interested in the East–West conflict, leading on from the Second World War, and we used to discuss all those big issues.

I don't think my mother was so politically interested, but she joined in the discussions. I finished my sixth-form year and didn't quite know what I wanted to do. I got a very bad appendicitis attack and my mother said, 'You're not going to fluff around in the seventh-form year.' It was her analysis that seventh form was a wasted year. After I became better I started Massey University, which meant I was actually very young.

I was above average, but I was never top of the class. But she pushed me and I think that helped a lot. I lived at home in Feilding and travelled to Palmerston North each day. I was never involved in the university politics of the student union, that didn't really appeal to me. I was more interested in the international affairs that were going on. After a year at Massey I came to Wellington and was at Victoria. We protested against the Vietnamese War in front of Parliament. I thought the National Government were allies of the US and basically conservative old Tories.

I left university and wanted to work in a trade union. Basically the doors were closed to me because I was young, female, and university-educated. I went through a period of unemployment, then I took up a clerical job to earn money and I did a bit more industrial relations study at Victoria University. The first job that I really wanted to get into was as a research worker with the Industrial Commission, which was the equivalent of the Employment Court. I worked there in industrial relations but from the middle ground, not from the union point of view.

After working for them and ranting and raving on about all sorts of issues of the day, my boss said to me, 'What you need is a bit of good practical experience. Why don't you go off and be a factory inspector?' I said, 'Okay, I will.' So I did. He probably got a bit sick of me theorizing about it. But I really enjoyed it, and it did give me a very good practical grounding in what went on in workplaces and the relationship between employers and workers. Then a job came up with the Clerical Union. By this stage I had a bit of experience under my belt. I was still a young, university-educated female and that was a bit of a downer, but I eventually got into the trade union.

When I'd originally gone around the unions, the Federation of Labour was housed in the old Trades Hall and it was like going back to the fifties. It was very depressing. They had a very elderly research worker there who basically did nothing.

Therese O'Connell was the first woman to be employed at the Clerical Workers' Union, and it was through her that I got the job. She's a wonderful lady, and I became the second woman to be employed. We encouraged more and more women, to the extent that by the time I left we were ninety per cent female employees of the union, also reflected in the executive, the elected body of the union. It became very representative of its membership.

In addition to the Clerical Union, women's involvement in the movement started in the Shop Employees', then filtered through to the Distribution Union when they amalgamated, and then the Service Workers' Union, which is mainly female membership. There was always Sonja Davies, of course, of the Shop Employees', but she came in during a much earlier period. The real movement of women coming in was more around my time. By then Sonja was working for the FOL.

It was pretty difficult for us; a classic case of not being taken seriously. One point where that became noticeable was around 1983 when Muldoon introduced voluntary unionism. Having talked about it for many years, he actually introduced the bill and brought it in. Women in the Clerical Union knew what the impact of that was. We knew our union would virtually disappear under that system, and we knew the vulnerability of those women members.

There was quite a significant meeting which we called with other trade unionists where we laid out our fears, and said that as a trade union movement we had to fight this measure. A lot of the feedback from the male unionists who'd been around for a long time—including back to the '51 dispute—was that this was a chance for the union movement to get rid of the shackles of the legislative constraints. They saw no real need to oppose it and there was a big stand-off between us and the Clerical Union.

We were angry because we received feedback that we were just being hysterical females. That was a bit of a turning-point in understanding. And we've been absolutely vindicated by that. It was a difference in attitudes between the men and the women.

Annette King

. . . I was drilling teeth one day and I was a Member of Parliament the next, with little preparation at all for entering Parliament.

I grew up in a very traditional extended family. My grandfather lived with us for about a decade, and before that our grandparents lived next door. My father and mother both worked as office employees. Murchison was a very safe little town, a very insular little place. A place where you never locked doors and all those things, and you went visiting the cemetery on Sunday, followed by visiting one of your friends or relatives.

My mother and father were strong Labour. My father had a long tradition of Labour in his family. His family came out to the West Coast as miners from Jarrow. They all came out here as miners to places like Denniston and Millerton and Granity. Then my grandfather shifted to Murchison to work in the coal-mine. My father worked in the mines for a year before he went into the Post Office. My grandfather became a National Party supporter in old age, so he used to have some great barneys with my father over politics. Before that, for years and years, he was a roadman for the Ministry of Works.

Fran Wilde encouraged me to stand for politics. I joined the Labour Party in Hamilton in 1972 when Labour won the election, and I shifted down to Wellington in 1981 and joined Fran's electorate committee. She and Helen Clark encouraged me to stand. The contacts I got at that stage were really from Fran, who had been a researcher at Parliament for a long time.

They were looking for women to stand in seats, and within the party there was a drive to select more women; there still is. Initially Fran encouraged me to put my name in for Tasman, which included Murchison, when Bill Rowling announced he was going to stand down. That was in 1983. So I went into a campaign down there to win the nomination.

I spent a month or so campaigning around the area, and Fran Wilde helped me write my original speech—as she's helped a lot of people I know, like Liz Tennet and Trevor Mallard. Over the years she's been a really important person who's helped people getting into Parliament.

It was very funny, because she came down for the selection and she and I were staying in a motel together. About an hour before the selection she decided to change part of my speech and I didn't want to change it. I said to her afterwards the reason that I did so badly was that she changed my speech. It wasn't the reason at all. I didn't have a show of winning, because Sir Wallace Rowling told me himself that a woman could not win in a seat like Tasman.

I wasn't going to stand again. I thought that's it, it was a horrible experience. I think it might have been Helen Clark that second time who said, 'Why don't you put your name in for Horowhenua?' It was just up the coast and it was marginal. I think Geoff Thompson held it by 800 and something.

I was surprised when I won it. I hardly had a chance to get campaigning because Muldoon called a snap election. I was a tutor here at the dental school and I left at the beginning of the May holidays and Muldoon called an election in June. In July I was elected, so I often say I was drilling teeth one day and I was a Member of Parliament the next, with little preparation at all for entering Parliament.

Margaret Moir, MP for West Coast, 1990–.

I knew that I was going to have a heavy workload but I was used to working hard anyway. I'd been friendly with Fran long enough to know that any personal time she had was was snatched between working in Parliament and working in the electorate. But I love it. The initial drive for any of this sort of thing is politics. I love to talk politics, to breathe politics.

Margaret Moir

I'd only ever been in the House once to peer down and look at the people who were in that debating chamber.

I'm from the West Coast, which has traditionally been seen as very much a male place, and I think it still is. It's a shootin', huntin', fishin' style place, and it is definitely more of a male society than a female one. Generally, if a woman is going to get ahead she has to stand up for herself more. As a woman who's become more involved in local body politics I found you have to prove yourself and your ability. It's not just accepted.

I got involved in politics when I lived in Franz Josef. I lived there for seventeen years and I was heavily involved in the community. One of our local county councillors was moving away and trying to get somebody else to stand. Typically, I went around to every man I could think of who might stand, but I couldn't find anybody who wanted to do it and I was really quite disappointed. My husband Derek said, 'Why the hell don't you give it a go?' I honestly hadn't thought about it, but I did stand in the end.

Derek and I owned a motorcycle shop in Hokitika until about a year ago. I was still heavily involved in it, even when I became an MP, but I found I was working there on Sundays, going into the shop to do the books, the GST, the wages, the Inland Revenue requirements, and so on. But Derek wasn't there on Sundays. I said to him, 'This is crazy. You're there all week, I'm there at the weekend. We actually need to spend a bit of time together.' So we ended up selling the shop.

I was a pretty naïve politician when I entered the House. I didn't have a preconceived idea of what it was like. I'd only ever been in the House once to peer down and look at the people who were in that debating chamber.

Judy Keall

'Look Keall . . . either put up or shut up.'

Thinking back on it, I was finally motivated to get involved during the end of the Muldoon years. In 1980 there was a by-election where Wyn Hoadley stood. She became Mayor of Takapuna later on, but she stood for Labour in the East Coast Bays by-election when Mr Gill retired. I thought she was a good, strong woman candidate and I helped her, had a cottage meeting, went door-knocking, that sort of thing.

She missed out, and afterwards I went around saying, 'Why didn't the Labour Party do this?' and 'Why didn't the Labour Party do that?' One day one of my friends stopped me in my tracks and said, 'Look Keall, you're not even a member of the Labour Party. Either put up or shut up.' So I went to a meeting and signed up because I was really concerned Muldoon had got so bad. Then in 1981 it was the Springbok tour and I got really stuck in because it just seemed like he was dividing the whole country.

I was part-time teaching in the late seventies, but then as I became involved in politics I took on relief teaching because it was easier to fit in the political work. There was this new seat at Glenfield and on paper it was a marginal National seat.

Lorraine Wilson was a member of the Labour Women's Council, a group that has always taken very seriously the need for affirmative action for women in Labour Party politics. She rang me up and said that there were five men who'd been nominated for Glenfield and she was very concerned that there were no women because it was a marginal seat.

She and I decided we'd try and find some suitable women candidates. We asked a lot of people, and for one reason or another they were not available. In the end we decided we would both accept nominations. So we went into it together basically to fly the flag for women. We felt there needed to be more women in Parliament and so that's how I came to stand.

I didn't expect to get the selection but, as it came closer, I realized that I was one of only two local candidates, so I did prepare for the selection meeting very carefully. Then, as we did our door-knocking conscientiously and we got back the responses I became more and more confident. The party certainly didn't expect to win it, but by election day I was pretty sure that we could do it if we got all the Labour Party supporters out to vote. There was a big swing and I got in by 800 votes.

Note

1. Margaret Shields won Kapiti in the 1978 election with an 'on-the-night' majority of seven votes which increased to fifteen after the counting of special votes. Her National opponent, Barry Brill, sought and was granted a magisterial recount on the grounds that there were inconsistencies in the way some voters had registered their choices on their ballot papers. The magistrate's interpretation of the electoral law regarding voters' intentions led to the overturning of the election-night result and produced an eighty-three-vote majority for Brill. Shields petitioned the Supreme Court to overturn this decision, but abandoned her petition in the light of the 'ticks and crosses' judgment in respect of a similar controversy in the Hunua electorate.

2

FAMILY LIFE

When someone becomes an MP, their life changes radically. Most of their week is spent in Wellington, and the electorate keeps them busy on the other days. If they have children they may be fortunate enough to have a few hours of 'family time' on Sundays. Separation is a fact of life, even if they are from a Wellington electorate. They will often leave for work before the children are up and be home after midnight when the children are in bed.

Some women have opted not to have children; others have delayed seeking selection until they thought their children were old enough to cope. Many of the MPs interviewed said that, without strong support from their partners and families, the job would be virtually impossible.

Ruth Richardson

> *. . . I had a six-week-old baby and a House sitting on my hands.*

I made a conscious decision not to have children until I had become a parliamentarian. I felt that the hurdles facing a young woman seeking a safe seat were substantial enough. It represented enough of a challenge without adding the dimension of children. Once I'd secured myself in a seat it was an appropriate time then to be able to make a decision.

The two things in my favour were very good health during those pregnancies and, with that, an extremely supportive family environment— family and friends were very, very supportive. So it was a very positive environment with strong support. The second thing that worked for me was the political support of my colleagues who on both occasions were very helpful.

In the House, particularly the Whips, Don McKinnon and Michael Cox, were superb. And I had leaders who were prepared to confer substantial responsibility on me. I was made a front-bencher and given the position of spokesman for my party for education, which was a substantial responsibility, pregnant to boot. So it was an extremely positive personal and political environment for me.

What was going against me on my first pregnancy was we were in the

Government and our majority was one. So the exceedingly slim nature of our majority introduced an element that was an extra risk to be managed.

I thought we'd been terribly clever in our family planning by having Lucy during the recess. They always have a number of public meetings around the electorate at the beginning of the year. I'd just finished a meeting at the public hall in Hororata. It was about ten o'clock. I was standing there talking to a couple of cockies and, the next minute, water all over the place. They didn't blink an eyelid. And Lucy was born within a few hours.

Anyway there was a decision to call an early session to validate legislation in the transport area. That basically threw my plan awry. Before the session started the Opposition denied me a pair.[1] Jonathan Hunt personally was very supportive, I've got to say. I think he was mortified by the decision that the women in his Caucus urged on him. It was women

Ruth Richardson, with her husband, Andrew, and her children, Lucy and Oliver, 1991.

primarily that took the view that I was not politically correct and therefore they were going to move against me. I think Jonathan was pretty embarrassed. He's a good soul. But there wasn't a similar element of goodwill among his female colleagues. They were able to operate in that sort of vindictive way because we had a majority of one. It meant I had a six-week-old baby and a House sitting on my hands. It was a logistical nightmare. Lucy got colic; Andrew was holding down a lecturing job at Lincoln.

Lucy had to be with me, of course. We had to fly our child-care worker up each week and board her in a hotel, but she could only work so many hours a day. So Andrew had to fly up at night and then he'd fly back in the morning. This happened for several days. I had a small box of a room as a back-bencher, so I was literally in one of the dog-boxes which were the habitation of back-bench MPs. Lucy obviously wasn't doing a hell of a lot of sleeping because I had a very disrupted schedule and consequently she became a very disruptive baby.

I breast-fed her for three to four full months, and the same with Oliver. It became difficult for both of them, having a home in Canterbury and my work in Wellington, but I gave them both the head start that they deserved. With my second pregnancy it was not such an issue because we were in Opposition and we were pretty much our own free agents. But Parliament at that time was a very hostile place for children, particularly small infants. It's become a much more inclusive place now.

The only other woman who had two children while in office was Whetu Tirikatene-Sullivan. Her children would often look after Lucy and Oliver when we were up at Bellamy's. When I was having the meal with the little ones, Whetu's son would trot Lucy and Oliver around. The Bellamy's staff were very good too, they would cart Lucy around in their time off.

Speaking of my daughter, Lucy has just given me a note: 'How long will you be on the phone—one minute, five minutes, ten minutes, fifteen, twenty, twenty-five? Circle the correct one.'

Whetu Tirikatene-Sullivan

During each of my pregnancies, it is a fact that other MPs took more sick-leave.

My husband and I have been blessed to rear our daughter, May-Ana, and our son, Tiri.

In between, a second daughter, Lise-Marie, was born prematurely and survived in an incubator under intensive care at Wellington Hospital until she died from an unexpected infection at three months old. It took some years before I came to terms with that deep wrench in my life.

None of my colleagues would have known anything about that, although for the three months of her life, I used to spend my lunch and dinner hours by her incubator, occasionally being able to hold her in my arms. She got to know my voice and used to respond. She was so tiny and so precious.

Our society has yet to demonstrate how precious children are: so many die needlessly because of carelessness. It is an immense responsibility to rear them well. Yet, new parents are not taught how to manage.

Denis and I wanted to have children, and so we were prepared to put quality time into our personal care of them. From personal experience, I can share with other caring parents how much of the day goes on ensuring one's children are well cared for. It is in the nature of women to soldier on through long, fatiguing days, managing pregnancy with its discomforts and increasing fatigue; coping well into the evening with all the rest of the household management. An eighteen-hour day.

Even then, since we were both professionals, we had the support of a third person, Rona. Any other support has to be regular, continuous, and consistent: ideally, the same person. Rona was all this to us.

However, Denis and I cared for our first-born, May-Ana, totally ourselves for the first four months. We took her in her carry-cot between home and my office at Parliament; and with us as we travelled the length and breadth of Southern Māori.

When May-Ana was four months old, Rona called to my office at Parliament. She followed events in the media and had come to ask if she could care for May-Ana whenever I was working, although she did not immediately reveal this to me.

On cue, May-Ana began to cry—the first time she had, other than for her bottle—so Rona offered to take her for a walk. However, she first learnt of my intention to retire from politics at the next election. When Rona returned, she had a second request: 'Please don't leave Parliament. We need you there, to fight for us. I can care for your baby during the day.' She said the same when Tiri was born.

Denis and I would pack all their needs—nappies, clothes, food, and drink—and deliver the freshly bathed children. She loved them, as she had her own grandchildren, and they cherished her right until her recent death. They were with her family at her hospital bedside. The previous weeks, they had taken her out for drives, to restaurants, and taken her flowers and other treats. The cherishing was mutual.

I was the first woman in New Zealand to bear a child while a sitting MP—and, in Tiri's case, the first Cabinet minister. During the weeks before May-Ana was born, Parliament was meeting literally around the clock. (There was no such thing as a break between midnight and 9 a.m.) However, I missed no divisions.

My parliamentary leader was Norman Kirk. As Leader of the Opposition, we had had some major arguments. For instance, he phoned to stop a broadcast I was about to make on the state of New Zealand's race relations. The station manager was aghast at such an intrusion. But when Norman became Prime Minister, he was more relaxed—and very understanding. We got on very well, from then on.

He was very thoughtful when I was expecting May-Ana and respected that I soldiered on, taking only six working days off Parliament for her birth. He insisted on requesting Mabel Howard's footstool from the Parliament basement, so I could at least 'put my feet up' in Parliament. No one could really notice it, and I certainly benefited from it.

He said he had learnt, from his wife, the importance of such a footrest during pregnancy. Caucus insisted I attend with my infant, to whom they presented an inscribed silver cup. I was delighted. I felt I should keep on at my job to demonstrate to my fellow parliamentarians that pregnancy was not a disability which afflicted women MPs. In fact, during each of my pregnancies, it is a fact that other MPs took more sick-leave.

I took six working days off when May-Ana was born and, in an urgent moment, was rushed from Bethany Salvation Army Hospital to Wellington Hospital for an unexpected surgical delivery. Denis, who had been at my bedside, insisted on carrying me in his arms to our car and driving me over. As with each of my caesarian deliveries, he waited outside the theatre to accompany me as I was wheeled on a stretcher back to the ward. I used to regain consciousness on the trip back along the corridors of Wellington Hospital, and he would tell me what the surgeon had told him about our babe's birth. We had great respect for Mr Corkill.

I designed swirling caftans and ponchos with bold Māori motifs. Tiri was born when I was a minister. Wearing one of my original ponchos, I accompanied Norman and Ruth Kirk to what was to be his last public function. Both of us had felt great pain that day, but the photos do not indicate this as we went about that busy 'official visit' to Feilding.

Among the many well-wishers, two organizations stood out: the Māori Women's Welfare League and the New Zealand Māori Council, both of which expressed admiration at the way I continued my advocacy of a Māori viewpoint in crucial debates in Parliament despite my pregnancy. I was referred to as 'Wāhine Toa'.

On the other hand, I was bitterly criticized by a couple of groups who described themselved as 'feminists' for ruining their case for matrimonial leave. That was to be the first of a stream of similar letters I have received from such groups.

Competent parenting and home management are the most complex and demanding twin roles. My experience had led me to admire competent family managers and homemakers; and also men who help in the task when they can (as my own father did).

When I have given public expression to this admiration, I have inevitably attracted bitter comment from the same groups who criticized me for not taking maternity leave.

I have learnt to distinguish such women by the venom in their attack. They have also, unwittingly, attacked my Rātana background with its uncompromising Christian origin.

After the swearing-in of the Labour Cabinet, December 1972. Whetu Tirikatene-Sullivan at right. New Zealand Herald

Helen Clark

*I take my hat off to people who can add their own
families and family concerns on top of that, but I just
don't think I could happily do it.*

Having children has never been something I've wanted to do because I value
my personal space and privacy too highly. I cannot think of the sort of life I
would want to have where I would want to give up those things for children.
I've observed many friends and relatives with children over many years, and
nothing that I've seen has led me to change my mind. I don't think it's just
this job. I think that anything that I did I would have been very busy, and
when I wasn't putting a lot into it I would have wanted personal space for
myself. The other thing is, I spend my whole life working with and on behalf
of people. I can't go to work and just shut the door on people and their
concerns: that is the job. I take my hat off to people who can add their own
families and family concerns on top of that, but I just don't think I could
happily do it.

Elizabeth Tennet

*Isn't that just typical?—they can pay for a bloody sauna,
but they can't pay for a centre that helps all the women
who work in this place.*

I didn't have any children when I stood, and I knew that to have a child as an
MP you've got to plan your whole life around that and make sure that it
works. Otherwise you become a very ineffective Member of Parliament. My
son was born in November and I went back to work in February and we have
had a child-minder since then.

My husband's always been very helpful, and he takes over the night-shift.
We've just got to plan everything down to the last quarter-hour. I pushed for
the crèche in Parliament. Initially it kept being put off. It was approved under
the Labour Government. Had there not been a change of government, it
would have gone ahead in 1990 or very quickly in 1991. But that delayed it.

There was a period there where a decision was made not to go ahead with
it. I think that was through the Parliamentary Services Commission, which
runs the budgeting service for the running of Parliament, based on a drop in
allocations they were given from the government at large. But then with a
bit more funding, and I suspect even a bit of push from the National women
in Cabinet, it was decided to go ahead with it.

It's even more difficult for women in Parliament who don't live in Wellington to have children. I really wonder how Ruth Richardson managed with her children, especially in those very young days. When they're very young it's really hard. I organized the routine of the breast-feed around my committee meetings and the programme of the day. My son was a very good baby. I now realize he was a one out of a hundred and I was very lucky.

He's my only child, and if I wasn't an MP I'd probably have another one. But because I am an MP I've decided not to. It is very tiring, especially in the first year. If I didn't have such a good baby the second time, I don't know how I'd cope. He's a very good sleeper. I think he's one of the twenty per cent that are. He slept all night every night from the time he came home and I just thought that was normal baby behaviour. I now realize it's not.

The room we used was an old office. It was actually used by Roger Douglas when he was kicked out of Cabinet, so it had a little bit of history attached to it. It was most inadequate for a baby. We brought in a mobile cot and put up colourful things around the walls. But it was adjacent to two walkways and so everybody walking up and down immediately woke Matthew.

Ultimately we got the crèche. We had an official little gathering and celebration. There was a slight tussle about who we would get to be the speakers. I made it very clear that if the National Party hogged the speaking list I would be most upset because I felt that I'd done more than any of them to get the crèche.

So it was agreed that the Speaker would be the official number one speaker. Then Jenny Shipley spoke as Minister of Women's Affairs and I spoke representing the Labour Opposition. So that was fair enough. There was a great big cake. We had all the parents and quite a few others from Parliament at the official opening because it's open to all the staff.

I don't think it would have gone through if it was only open to children of MPs. That's the big difference between the approach Ruth Richardson made and the one that I made. When she talked about childcare she talked about having a separate room, whereas I talked about us having a crèche for the whole of Parliament.

There are 700 to 800 people who work up here and, as a good employer, it's our duty to provide that facility. I was able to argue under the Pay Equity and Equal Employment Opportunities legislation that the Labour Government had passed that year, that there was a requirement on large employers to be good employers and to provide opportunities for women. I said that, if they didn't provide a crèche, I would be looking to take a legal case against Parliament for not being a good employer and not providing equal employment opportunities. I said that to the manager of the Parliamentary

Services Commission, Mr Brooks, and I think that put the wind up him.

No one actually opposed it. It was just something that wasn't important. What made me angry was the shift over to the new building. There had been

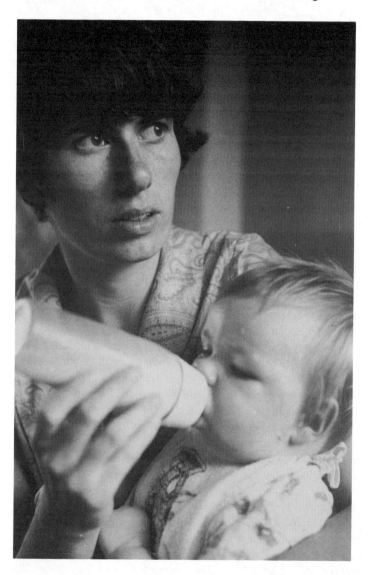

Fran Wilde, MP for Wellington Central, 1981–92, feeding her eldest child, Stephen.

a suggestion made by some of the male MPs—it certainly didn't come through any of the processes—that they put a sauna into this building for the MPs. I thought: 'Isn't that just typical?—they can pay for a bloody sauna, but they can't pay for a centre that helps all the women who work in this place.'

So I did my grumble over that. There was a bit in one of the papers once about how the workers at Parliament, because they worked at Parliament, expected something special that the rest of the population didn't have. And how much it would cost Parliament. I made some repy like, 'It's funny how they can provide the baths and the swimming pool and all these other facilities for people, but when it comes down to a basic working issue for women, it's considered a real cost.'

Lianne Dalziel

. . . what do you do with the baby? You'd virtually have
to move to Wellington . . .

I don't know how people have children with this job. Elizabeth Tennet had a child while she was in Parliament and I take my hat off to her, but she's a Wellington-based member and I think that's probably about the only way you could do it. Whetu did it. Ruth Richardson did, and I do not know how they did it.

I'm sure my husband would be willing to take over parental duties if we wanted to have children, but that's not the issue. The issue is whether you actually physically could deal with it.

You can't fly on a plane—I think it's a month before—the airlines won't touch you. So that's a month out of your working time. Then there's afterwards, and what do you do with the baby? You'd virtually have to move to Wellington, I guess. I don't know.

Sonja Davies

I said, 'Where's the child-care centre?' They just looked
at me in horror. And Hawke said, 'We can't have one
here . . . '

I just feel terrible for the people who have had babies in here, Ruth Richardson included. There were no facilities. We've got a crèche now, but that finishes at five o'clock, and this place goes on till half-past ten.

In Australia they haven't got one at all. I'm very unpopular, because twice I've gone over and taken them on about that. They took me around and showed me the spa pool and the self-emptying, self-filling swimming pool, the squash courts, and the gymnasium with the exercycles, and all the other things. And the bank and the shops. I said, 'Where's the childcare centre?' They just looked at me in horror. And Hawke said, 'We can't have one here because that would give the message to employers that they ought to do it too.' I said, 'Well, yes, that's the idea.'

Whetu Tirikatene-Sullivan, Liz Tennet, and Ruth Richardson all had babies after they were elected. They all had supportive husbands and families, but it was still difficult. Ruth Richardson has been quite fortunate that she's got a very supportive husband who loves Oliver and Lucy and will take his share. But nevertheless there are times when I'm sure she'd rather be with Oliver, when he's not well and when he goes to school. They get out of school at two o'clock for the first little while. What happens after school? What happens in the holidays? This place isn't geared for any of that at all. I really think it's still an old boys' club and the very young boys get into that. I think if they were honest they wouldn't like it.

Geoffrey Palmer introduced recesses to coincide with the school holidays so that people could be with their kids. But that's as far as it's ever gone. I think if they had half women they'd say, 'This doesn't suit. We can get through as much if not more work if we fit it in with our families.' Because at the moment I would hate to have a family and be in here.

Katherine O'Regan

[Marilyn Waring] was asked, 'What would you do if you got married?' Her reply was, 'You wouldn't ask me that if I was a man.'

I think the crèche works well, but it's mostly for staff. It must be very difficult for a woman who's breast-feeding babies or having to look after little ones. Personally, I don't think you can do both, but it's a matter of choice. When I was first nominated my children were too young.

Of course women have that placed on them constantly. Christine Fletcher was told, 'Oh you should be at home with your children.' The first time I ever heard anything like that was with Marilyn Waring. She was asked, 'What would you do if you got married?' Her reply was, 'You wouldn't ask me that if I was a man.'

At that stage my own feminism was probably only embryonic. I'd always

Katherine Newton (later Katherine O'Regan, MP for Waipa, 1984–) as a student nurse.

had very strong heroines like Elizabeth Fry and Florence Nightingale. Marilyn was really a catalyst for my own feminism. I think she extended the views of everyone in her electorate. I would probably not agree with her on economics, but as a good friend and as a woman who knows a lot about other women and how women are, she's second to none.

Marilyn is probably the only real feminist I know who has no party political leaning at all and is purely pro-women. It's a great advantage to have a friend like that. She was wonderful to work for in those eight years and she taught me a lot. I hope that I managed to teach her some things that perhaps she didn't know much about, particularly in the areas of local government and in some life experiences which she'd never had. But I've never experienced the antipathy she did.

When my marriage broke up I was deeply worried as to how people would see it in my electorate, but I received nothing but the kindest comments and understanding. I was quite amazed. People would say to me, 'Don't worry Katherine, it's happened to my family too', 'my daughter's going through a bad patch', or, 'I'm on my second marriage.' I was really very grateful for the kindness that people showed me during that time. I thought it would be much harder for a woman going through a break-up of a marriage

Margaret Austin

I was ostracized by my neighbours as being neglectful.

I remember saying to my father when I was about to marry in 1955 that I thought that I would probably be lucky to spend ten years being domesticated. In the event, I spent six years in two three-year stints.

I gave up work for a little while just before the first was born, and then we went overseas on leave, came back, and had another daughter. I went back for half a day each five days a week when Nicola was ten weeks old. 1959 that was. I was ostracized by my neighbours as being neglectful; I was criticized by my in-laws for being totally out of kilter with the rest of society.

Fortunately my own parents were supportive. And it worked very well. It was right in the middle of the intense science teacher shortage, and I had the

Margaret Austin with her children, Faith, Nicola, and Mark, February 1967.

opportunity to do senior chemistry and senior biology—too good an opportunity to miss.

I had married a university teacher. He was totally supportive and I wasn't trained to teach chemistry so I was very dependent on a lot of input from him to get me up to speed.

Then I had another; the youngest was born in 1961. I spent three years being at home and I went back again and did further part-time for another two years and took a full-time appointment in 1966. I employed a woman whose family was grown up who was prepared to devote herself to my children. And so I earned nothing at all, but that was not important. The important thing was that I felt satisfied.

I got great joy and satisfaction out of the children, but at the same time I had two streams to my life. You know the greatest thrill was you had the challenge and the stimulation of the classroom, but also the tremendous joy from having watched your own children grow up to be articulate, independent, and able to make the same sorts of commitments that I made.

I remember being dressed down by one neighbour one day because I was training our four-year-old to cross a quite busy street to do a simple errand. And I was being totally irresponsible and reckless. But I've always believed—why should you answer a child's question if you can lead them through a series of observations so that they arrive at the answer themselves? I suppose it's the teacher in me, but it always seems to be a cop-out to answer someone's question directly, particularly a young person, if you think they can arrive a conclusion that they feel is their own as a result of what they know and observe.

Judith Tizard

My mother had four children in five-and-a-half years. She came to her senses eventually. And we're all grateful it wasn't before us.

I've made a conscious decision not to have children. I like children and I think I would be a good parent, and I think I would enjoy being a parent. But I can't see any way you can do both. If I were a Wellington MP I might think about it, but that's probably the main thing I've given up to go into Parliament. I'm not saying absolutely no, I've still got reasonable time to think about it. But I can't see how I could do what I do and have children. I guess I do give up a lot of my social life, because I just don't have time.

I'm the third of four. I have two older sisters and a younger brother. And then I have a half-brother as well, who is eleven. In our family there were the big girls, my sisters, and then there were the little ones, who were my brother and me. We're all very close; my mother had four children in five-and-a-half years. She came to her senses eventually. And we're all grateful that it wasn't before us.

She was very busy. She went back to university in 1960, so I was just at school, literally that month; and my brother went to kindergarten just across the river from my grandfather. My grandfather used to go and pick him up, and then Mum would pick them up and it was all very complicated. Then she got a part-time job which became a full-time job, and she was always tremendously busy, doing neighbourhood things, which then developed into suburb-wide and city-wide and so on.

I used to spend a lot of time cooking and fiddling around at home, and I spent a lot of time with my grandparents. On holidays Nigel and I would often go to my grandparents and I spent a lot of weekends. It was a very busy house. For the whole of my memory Dad was in politics. I think I remember the 1957 election, but it may just be that I've heard the stories so often that it's just that I think I can remember. 1960, when he lost, I can remember quite well. I can remember the stench of defeat. Catastrophic.

I was often the home person; I did the organizing and sort of support stuff at home. I've always done that, and I became very close to my parents when my sisters left home and Nigel and I were left. I think place in the family is terribly important, about the way you perceive the world and what you see as your role, and I was just sort of born and brought up being a busybody, really.

It seems to me that my instincts are very political, but I guess if I was the child of doctors I may have gone into medicine and seen the problems of the world in medical terms. But they were both politicians, and that was always the major focus of our family. It's a very personal thing. Mum's great line is that she went to a meeting and told them what she thought they ought to do and she was on the committee. I feel strongly that you have no right to criticize if you haven't tried to change it.

You spend a lot of time just talking with people in a very sort of tense and immediate way. I have to respond to often quite oblique messages that I receive. Somebody who tells me that they're a bit unhappy may well be suicidal. Somebody who's got a bit of a family problem may be telling me that their housing situation is causing absolute crisis.

As a new MP, it seems to me important that I work out the personal things early on, and how I want to operate. My father was a very personal politician. Most people would not perceive him as that, but talking to people in the Panmure electorate it's been quite extraordinary: 'Bob Tizard called around here one morning on his way to the airport and the next day our windows were fixed', or 'we got a transfer', or 'he had a talk to my son and he went back to school and now he's a doctor.' So people see the MP as having an effect on their lives in a very personal way.

Marie Hasler

. . . I've always had jobs I put a lot into.

I had good teachers. I was taught by nuns, but they were mostly well-educated women and reasonably independent. I notice that a lot of the other women MPs are from girls' schools too. You probably get the opportunity for more leadership roles in an all-girls school.

I've personally known several politicians, and I noticed that they all worked hard. It certainly is a demanding job. But I've always had jobs I put a lot into. I haven't got children, so my work has been my hobby. I'm used to quite a hectic pace. Although the hours are very long, I was able quickly to adjust.

Annette King

. . . always having to be second fiddle would be awful.
I'd hate to be the husband or wife of a politician.

I'd separated before I came to Wellington to be a tutor here, but it wasn't helped by my political involvement. I just don't know how marriages survive. If you're an MP, you're always apart. And when the person does come home they've got to continue working in the electorate and they're pretty worn out anyway. I don't know where the energy is to maintain a relationship. They've got to be superheroes to do it. Some do it very well, and they've got very understanding wives and husbands who carry the burden of bringing up the family and doing all the work—garden, house, the whole lot. Those sorts of things you rarely get a chance to do. And always having to be second fiddle would be awful. I'd hate to be the husband or wife of a politician.

I'm not sure whether, as an MP, I've had specially hard times with my daughter Amanda. Looking at all my friends' children, when they reach teen age it's hard anyway. I think Amanda has had some hard times, rather than me. I think it's been harder for her than other kids. Sometimes I feel really bad about that.

She was fourteen when I went into Parliament. I had a woman come in and live here for when I was away at the weekends in Horowhenua. There were lots of things I didn't get to go to, like when Amanda got into the water polo championships. Just not being there for her. Every now and then you'd sense her frustration at the job I had. How she hated it when she heard things about me. She wouldn't want to own up to who her mother was in case they said something to her.

But she's twenty-three now, and she's now busy running my canvassing. I didn't think she'd ever actually get interested in politics. She was so sick of always people at the house, always people talking politics, always the phone going. She'd never want anything to do with them. Then recently, when I really needed someone to help me because the person who was doing it went away, she said, 'I'd like to do that job.' She's been brilliant. So she might be on the path to being interested in politics after all.

Margaret Moir

I couldn't even conceive of combining having a young family with being an MP . . .

My children are twenty-six and twenty-four. They've left home. Tracey, the younger, is over in the Channel Islands on a working holiday and my son Glenn lives in Christchurch. I think that they were a little bit embarrassed when I went into politics but certainly they're very proud now. But they still don't necessarily disclose that their Mum's an MP unless they're actually probed, which is interesting.

I couldn't even conceive of combining having a young family with being an MP, especially as a mother. I know that there are mothers and fathers who are in Parliament with young children, but I think it must be a really difficult thing to judge what your priorities are, at times. Your priority as a mother would always be your family, but when you're an MP your family really doesn't come off best.

My advice to someone who is young and perhaps considering entering politics would be: talk to some MPs and establish from them how it's affected their lives. Discuss what your concerns are with them and realize that you have to allocate a huge amount of time to your job. But I guess it doesn't matter what advice anybody gives you, if you're determined to do it, you'll do it. Just be aware of the sacrifices you have to give to the job as a person.

Joy McLauchlan

. . . you're not sure you want to have an in-depth conversation with your baby at two in the morning.

From a personal perspective, I am glad that my children were older when I was successful. That's because I'm quite possessive about my children and when they were growing up—my kids would be the first to agree with this—I wanted to be around them and near them as much as possible. When they got older, beyond those formative years, that was fine. But from a personal point of view I would not have liked to have been in Parliament when my children were preschool or even through until high school years. But I don't point the finger at anyone who's made that decision to do that, these are just my feelings.

The sense of reward and fulfilment for me, having the children has just been immeasurable. So I do feel very sorry for those people who make a conscious decision not to, but that's their right to make that decision. I know that, with some of my male colleagues particularly, there have been a number who have become fathers since we've been in Parliament, maybe for the second or third time, maybe for the first time. It is difficult for them to spend that bonding time that we talk about.

Even when the House is not sitting you're still involved in meetings. There's this general perception out there that we only work three days a week, three weeks a month sort of thing, and that is totally inaccurate. When the House is not sitting we're probably busier than ever in terms of time spent at meetings, and being lobbied, whatever. There are very few free evenings. You might get home at 11 p.m. rather than, say, two in the morning. I suppose a baby could well be awake then, but you're not sure you want to have an in-depth conversation with your baby at two in the morning.

Anne Collins

'There's a stranger in the lobby.'

It was always sort of bubbling away. I can remember once my daughter was with me in the visitors' lobby in Parliament and we'd had some sort of agreement to meet at five o'clock or something and it went on and on. Trevor Young took a point of order saying, 'There's a stranger in the lobby', and someone got up and said it was my daughter. And Jim Bolger got really

Anne Collins (Fraser), MP for East Cape, 1984–90, and daughter, outside Parliament. South Pacific News Ltd

nasty and spoke on a point of order and said basically I should be at home with the children where I belonged. So the feelings against women MPs were always just below the surface, it didn't need much to bring them out.

It's certainly harder if you've got little children, but I would imagine it would be harder for men if they wanted to take any sort of role in parenting as well. Women feel it more because we're more conditioned to the role of full-time mother than men.

Probably a Wellington seat wouldn't be so bad. These days there's a crèche. But still, it's a hell of a life for anyone with or without children. But I suppose, if I had my time over again and I wanted to be an MP, I guess I'd wait till my kids were a bit older.

It's so hard to just be a person. That's how I felt. Just after my marriage broke up, people started asking about *me*. It was such a shock, because it hadn't happened [before]. And I went to a women's meeting and they said, 'Look we don't want you here as an MP, just be yourself for the night.' And they just had a normal meeting and it was wonderful.

But the rest of the time, no matter what you did or where you went, you were an MP, your job was the most important. And that was really resented by your family.

When Bryce and I separated I was very apprehensive. It wasn't something that they would have chosen for me to do. But David Lange was fantastic, really supportive. He asked how Bryce was straight away. If he was being supported. And everyone was really good. Jonathan Hunt offered his house because I had nowhere to live basically. And that was lovely. You never, ever forget that sort of thing.

Letters came in through party people, particularly people who had been through marriage breakups. People were really good. Because it doesn't matter how much of a relief it is for people to get out of a relationship, there's still quite a long period of grieving. And a great sense of failure that you didn't manage to make something work that you said was going to be permanent. But my friends were pretty good. Michael [Cullen] had a much worse time than I did. My friends pretty well knew that Bryce was into a new relationship so they weren't so nasty.

It was very strange having to go back to Whakatane every weekend. I had to go home to pick up the children, then drive away every week and go to a rented place. That was hard.

Personally I did lose some friends; I think everyone does when they break up. Some people just can't help but take sides. But it was the right thing to do for me, it was the right thing for Bryce, and it was the right thing for the kids. It was much happier all round.

Judy Keall

It was quite strange coming home, and he'd call out 'Daddy' rather than 'Mummy'.

Stephen, my youngest, was only eight when I went in, and I think he's the one that probably did suffer from my absence. The other two were at secondary school so they were well on the way. Michael is the eldest, Christopher's the second one.

Graeme, my husband, was pretty supportive. I certainly didn't put my nomination in without his support. He was a schoolteacher, so he was able to be home after school for them, so there wasn't a problem that some people might have had in that sense. But I think my being away so much certainly made a difference to my relationship with Stephen.

It was quite strange coming home, and he'd call out 'Daddy' rather than

'Handing over the reins'—Annette King, MP for Horowhenua, 1984–90, with Judy Keall, Labour candidate for Horowhenua, 1993 and former MP for Glenfield, on the Foxton horse-drawn tram, January 1993.

'Mummy'. I realized that he related first to Graeme. But then that was good for Graeme, so maybe it was a bonus for him.

Funnily enough, when I was agonizing over whether or not to accept this nomination for Horowhenua they were all in favour of it. They encouraged me to do it. I suppose they knew I had missed the political life. And one part of me did. The other part of me was very relieved to be away from the long hours and hard work and the constant demands of so many people.

It's a very difficult thing to analyse. I missed my colleagues, of course, because when you've worked with the same group of people for a period of six years you do. But it was a relief to be able to get back to more normal life. To be able to spend a bit of time in the garden, to potter around the house, read books again, read novels, to listen to music again. I like jazz. I really love it.

Note
1   The granting of 'pairs' is a parliamentary convention whereby a party agrees

that one of its Members shall not vote in divisions, in order to compensate for the absence from Parliament of a Member of the opposite party. In this instance a refusal to grant a pair would have effectively reduced and could even have overturned the Government's majority—always a real threat during the Muldoon admistration of 1981–84.

3

LIFESTYLE

Politicians are often seen as having a sedentary lifestyle: sitting in the House, doing paperwork, appearing at press conferences. However, the reality is a life constantly on the move: from one appointment to the next, from one aircraft to another, shuttling through an endless string of engagements.

MPs spoke about the unhealthy lifestyle of working long hours with few breaks; of working in a high-stress environment in uncomfortable buildings with bad air-conditioning; of meals snatched between or during meetings. It's all a long way from the 'cushy life' that some people think MPs lead.

Jenny Shipley

I'm very fortunate, I've got the constitution of an ox.

When I first went in it was difficult. You wake up at night thinking about things and just get completely hyperactive in terms of, 'I must do this and I must do that.' When you're in Opposition you've got all that room because it is a much wider focus you're taking.

Any opportunity I was offered, I'd say yes to because I just was like a sponge and there was so much I wanted to know. And that exacerbated the problem to some extent. But I learnt to relax.

I work very hard. I'm at my office early in the morning; I try and leave there by eleven at night. I might be home at eleven and in bed at ten past and asleep at quarter past. I've come to the point that, having done what I can to try and make correct decisions, I can put it aside. Which allows me the space to relax and at least rest.

In a personal sense, I garden. I have a wonderful garden at home—well, I think it is . . . Gardens are wonderful. You put something in, they give something back.

There's a huge risk in politics that you don't look after yourself enough. I would be one of the better managers of time in the system and yet the biggest risk you run is not making time for yourself.

You need a system that eventually says, 'I am more important than this

Jenny Shipley with her husband, Burton.

meeting or that desperately important interview.' The system loads that on to you and things like blocking time in diaries and that can prevent it. I do that in terms of parts of the weekend—Sunday is a demarcation that I try and keep pretty clean in relation to the family and just having some space, but it's something I need to do more of.

I guess it's getting older, too—I used to always swim in the morning, and it's harder when you're forty to get out of bed and get into the water. But I love to swim and I'm still a very good swimmer.

I'm very fortunate, I've got the constitution of an ox and can stand enormous physical pressure. I've got a high tolerance to fatigue. But at the end of the day you do test your system if you don't keep yourself well. I probably do need to pay more attention to that. It's something I haven't managed that well, given the scale of the portfolios. But they're all excuses—at the end of the day no one's responsible for that except me.

There's a little pool in the bottom of Parliament and it's private. You don't perhaps appreciate how difficult privacy becomes. There is so little of my life that is private now. Some politicians are happy to go and physically exercise, you know, run the streets or whatever. That's fine, that suits them. For me, part of the relaxation of swimming is the actual privacy of it.

Helen Clark

I can fill up a hundred hours a week with work, but I'm not going to.

I've put in nine years of total dedication as an MP and an awful lot before that when I did very little with my free time except work for the Labour Party. There are some weeks still when I put in one hundred per cent of time, but I do make more personal space for myself now. I'm learning to speak Spanish. I go to the gym. I think I'm entitled to make time in my life for that. I don't accept every speaking invitation any more because it's not worth it, for me.

The interests that I personally have are listening to opera, going to opera, listening to music, going to concerts, going to films. I still have a large classical music collection but I find I'm listening to opera a lot more. My husband Peter is a jazz fan. He plays it when I'm out. I can't stand it. His taste in music is diametrically opposed to mine. He likes what I listen to, but I can't say that it applies the other way around. I'll come in after the electorate clinic on a Saturday. He'll have the house blasting.

So I've been reordering my priorities. I can fill up a hundred hours a week with work, but I'm not going to. What I'm finding very difficult in Opposition is the mail. If you're a high profile Opposition politician in areas of social policy where people are being badly hurt, the mail is horrendous.

All the letters have a story and they can't be brushed off. They've got to have a reply. You end up intervening on things like waiting lists all over the country because people have just got no where else to turn. You end up writing to an area health board about why is this person with painful gallstones not being seen? So the constituency has expanded enormously. It's a nationwide electorate.

We're trying to sort out a war pension problem in the south of the South Island. I remember one quite clearly over last year—it took almost a year to get money for a piece of equipment for a man in Northland in a little settlement. He just desperately needed it, and in the end, after many, many letters, somebody agreed to pay for it. He could never have done that on his own. You can delegate to an extent but the electorate office is full-time just on the local ones.

Annette King

When you're an MP you don't have time to spend with friends.

It's not a very healthy lifestyle. There were lots of things about myself I didn't like at the end—my size to start with. I was thin when I went into Parliament. It's a combination of factors. It's the way I put on weight. You have to be incredibly disciplined to fit exercise into your life. I'd never been a permanent exerciser because I'd always been thin and was always moving and never really put on much weight. But sitting in cars, sitting in planes, sitting in select committees—driving from Parliament to Levin several times a week. I just started with middle-age spread at an early age.

I can't blame Bellamy's. I didn't close my mouth when I should have, but it was also the lunches you have—things you wouldn't normally eat. Before I used to have a sandwich or some yoghurt or whatever. But as an MP your lunches would be sausage rolls because it was at some meeting—sausage rolls and deep-fried pieces of crumbed fish or something. So there was a lot of fat in my diet. Even though I've been out about two-and-a-half years and I've lost about two stone, I'm still too fat. So I haven't got back to my healthy lifestyle. I can't keep blaming the place.

When I lost my seat I did lie in bed for a little while. But it's not my nature, and so I was up and away again. I have enjoyed renewing old friendships and making new friends and doing things that I hadn't done for a long time.

If I return to Parliament I would continue doing some of those things, like ensuring that you do go out with friends and that you do see them, make time to have some social life of your own. When you're an MP you don't have time to spend with friends. But some people are long-suffering and, after I lost, people I hadn't seen for a long time phoned me up and said, 'Why don't you come and have a meal?' Next thing you know you're talking about old times and you're back where you started. They hadn't forgotten, where I might have found it harder to approach them because I'd been the one who had neglected them really.

Even though it's hard work it can be quite fun. There are some very humorous politicians. Some of the people that have been on these fun debates, when you see them in that forum they're very funny. I did quite a lot of them. I did one recently with David Lange and we had to joust against three schoolchildren, young adults, from colleges out in the Kapiti area. They cleaned us up good and proper. They were much better debaters. But the public love to see people making fools of themselves.

I had a reputation for the glasses I used to wear but I've given them away. Somebody coined this phrase, 'the Elton John of Parliament'. I've got contact lenses now. I became short-sighted late in life which isn't very common, and I hated wearing glasses. I decided that if I had to wear them then I was going to make them fun, so I used to go out and buy cheap sunglasses frames of any colour I could find and then have the lenses put in them. It was a very cheap option —about sixty dollars a time or something. Then I'd look in second-hand shops and scrounge the markets for unusual shaped frames.

Jenny Kirk

If you've been arguing with people all day, do you want to go and sit down to dinner with them?

The experience of being an MP was not what I expected. Totally. I didn't expect for instance that I would have to worry about my health. I found that, the way Parliament operates, you get very little time to care about yourself. I found after a while that I actually had to make quite firm rules for myself so that I kept fit and energetic.

There are ways in which you're put under pressure, so that your physical health suffers. For instance, the scheduling of meetings during mealtimes. And the food that was available at Bellamy's was quite fatty. Sometimes all the salads had meat in them. I'm not vegetarian, but if you're looking for some fresh greenery and you find it all chopped up with little bits of ham and salami, that's not really very good.

It had an effect on all of our health; we acknowledged we had health problems amongst ourselves. Exercise was one of my health priorities, so I developed strategies to deal with that stress. I walked to work, and I swam instead of going to those meetings during mealbreaks. We actually said no to the meetings.

I bought fresh fruit and vegetables. We bought a microwave and sometimes I used to cook there rather than eat Bellamy's food. This was also to get a break away from the people who caused the stress. If you've been arguing with people all day, do you want to go and sit down to dinner with them?

It was difficult to fit your own priorities into the parliamentary system. When you had a really important meeting in your electorate, you expected to be able to attend it. But you couldn't because you had to be voting fodder on some issue that you either didn't agree with or didn't think was very important. People who were sick had to have a doctor's note. People had to get the Whips' permission to go outside the House.

When the bells rang you had to drop everything and go into the House and vote. That might be even in the middle of select committee meetings where you had these people who had paid to come down to Wellington to make their important presentation. They expected to be treated as though they were important and being listened to. And I had to say to them, 'Oh, sorry, there's the bells, we've got to go.' They might be highly qualified people, professors, experts in their field. The bells rang and you had to say, 'Sorry, I have to go.' I thought that was really very rude to your constituents. It just seems to me there has to be a better way to run a country, rather than treating people like that. It was very like being back at school.

It was a very alien way of operating, not at all people-friendly. The stress involved in the economic direction of the Government—which is fundamentally opposed to the social direction of what I thought I was in there for—that was something I hadn't expected. I think actually thousands of women believed Labour's social policy and Labour lost a lot of women's votes; that's where I think they lost it.

Ruth Richardson

I wrote the 1992 Budget to Beethoven and called it 'Beethoven's Budget'.

I run every morning. This morning I went for a long bike ride. So I try and keep personally fit. In terms of any other leisure time I have, I spend it with my family, and in my garden. It's basically home, personal fitness, and that's all the time I've got.

Music? I used to listen to Patti Smith, Pink Floyd. I wrote the 1992 Budget to Beethoven and I called it 'Beethoven's Budget'. I like when I'm in a period of sort of intense concentration and really trying to be inventive and creative and look ahead. I like loud music. So it was Beethoven this last year.

Part of doing your job is travel. Often I will have breakfast in one city and lunch in another city and tea in another city. And you've got to be at your peak every time you get off the plane. Shortly, in thirty-six hours' time, I'll be flying to Tokyo. I'll be working there for two days and then in one day I will get up in Tokyo at six-thirty in the morning and fly for four hours to Hong Kong, work a day in Hong Kong, and then get on the plane and fly to Europe. Charming.

Part of my job is to go and see my bank managers; just like any other country or any other firm that's got a mortgage, you've got to keep your bank manager happy. New Zealand's bank managers are spread around the world and it's my job to go and keep contact with them. It's what I'll be doing for the next two weeks. Travel is not a perk. My family is here in Canterbury, my constituents are in Canterbury, my workplace is typically in Wellington, and my field work is typically both worldwide and New Zealand-wide. You've simply got to be on the move.

Marilyn Waring

To be allowed to say . . . 'Sorry, Sunday's nobody and nothing.' I didn't have that luxury.

Extraordinarily long hours. In those days before we were really conscious of smoke-free, we were frequently in smoke-filled rooms. There was little opportunity for exercise. Little respite. The winter period then was the constant sitting time. I understand now they break for school holidays. The debates where most of the urgency was taken were throughout that period.

Everybody would disperse to a different part of New Zealand for a weekend and everybody would bring back the regional lurgy and impose it on everybody else. So you could literally be recovering from one virus, get home from the weekend, and come back and catch Invercargill's version the next week. It was truly disgusting.

I found, as a woman who was understood to have no family obligations, that when I went home if I had said to anybody, 'Oh I'm sorry, this is my private day for my family', there would have been an outrage. I didn't have one so I wasn't supposed to have a day off.

I wasn't allowed any of that kind of comfort or privilege. Since I didn't have the standard heterosexual model to revert to, I had no excuses. To be allowed to say, as Ruth Richardson apparently does, 'Sorry, Sunday's nobody and nothing.' I didn't have that luxury.

Anne Collins

. . . I felt like I had my life back again.

The first time I went back to Parliament after I resigned, I felt like I had my life back again. It was a real burst of excitement. The first time I heard the bells and thought, 'I don't have to go in!' That was wonderful. Watching Parliament fill up from the gallery, and knowing I could just walk away and go and watch TV, or do whatever I wanted to. Wonderful!

Judy Keall

I used to walk to work and often walk home. I know I shouldn't have late at night, but I did.

Ironically I think I had a healthier lifestyle when I went in Parliament than when I first came out. I used to walk to work and often walk home. I know I shouldn't have late at night, but I did. When I was Junior Whip I always used

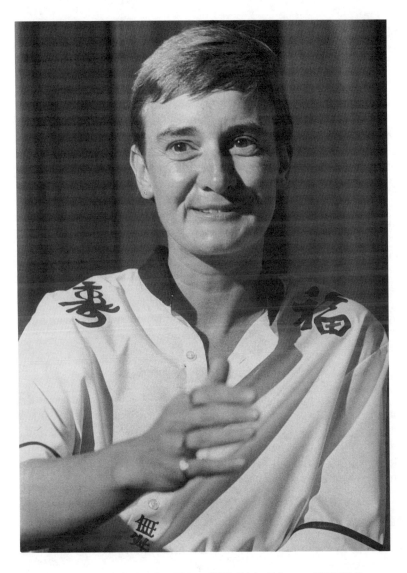

Marilyn Waring, MP for Raglan/Waipa, 1975–84, in February 1984. Waikato
Times

the stairs and not the lift. I was forever up and down, up and down, and I actually had a lot of exercise. I used to swim regularly as well.

When I came out of Parliament I got a job where I had to drive to work and drive back again and sit in an office all day. So I have been a bit different to other people in that respect.

Margaret Austin

You just have to get away . . .

You know something's wrong when you can't sleep at night. About once a year I'll probably go through a period of about a week where I have got myself wound up a bit and it takes me a couple of hours to get off to sleep.

When that happens I know that I've got to take time out and, whereas I do not leave here at night until my desk is clear, and I did that as a minister too, I try and sit back for a day or two and unwind.

There's only been Jack and I at home for a long time. Our youngest is now thirty-one, so long since gone. So we had a total role reversal: I take my washing home to him on the weekend and I come back here with a box of shortbread on a Tuesday morning. Because he bakes. I taught him.

For the last few years now I go to a gym in the mornings. I try to swim. My tracksuit is in the cupboard. I used to swim here but I haven't lately. But I swim in the public pool at home. That's really very good relaxation.

We go tramping in January; we've always taken our holidays in the mountains. Just to get out and walk and walk and walk for hours and hours on end. If you ask me how I cope, I'm prepared to devote myself to the work, but I insist on having the whole of January to myself. Absolutely insist. I close my study at home. It's got to be a real emergency to get me out because that's my time and you just have to get away.

Margaret Shields

. . . being a politician is one of the loneliest jobs on earth.

I always remember the advice that my husband Pat gave me when I first became a Cabinet minister. I was slightly overcome by the way in which people changed their behaviour towards me and the sort of things that went with the job. And Pat said to me, 'Don't be silly about this. This special treatment has nothing to do with you, it just goes with the job. Secondly it's temporary, no matter how long it lasts. And thirdly, enjoy it.' And so we did.

Hon. Margaret Shields, MP for Kapiti, 1981–90; Minister of Consumer Affairs, Minister of Customs, 1984–90; Minister of Women's Affairs, 1987–90.
Jocelyn Carlin

I think it's very important for any person entering politics, but particularly for women, to have a very clear idea of what they want to do and why they're doing it. It's very important to make sure that you can cope with the emotional problems of being in politics. Because you're going to be subjected to an enormous amount of criticism, no matter who you are or what you do. That means if you've got a family it's going to affect them. That's the sort of thing you really need to work through with your family.

You don't really know what it's like until it happens to you. Sort of like pain. Nobody can describe it to you. You have to experience it. A sense of humour is absolutely essential. But I think it's also important, particularly for women politicians, to realize that being a politician is one of the loneliest jobs on earth. There's people all around and it's as lonely as hell, because there are a lot of things you can't talk about with people, particularly if you're a Cabinet minister. And you really need people around who know you very well. And that becomes more, rather than less, important as time goes on.

You've got to have reality checks. And you've got to have people who know you well enough, for long enough, to know that if a decision comes out that seems to be against everything you have stood for, that you probably didn't vote for it. And that you are not really going to appreciate being ripped to shreds. Because you can't defend yourself. You've got to go out and defend the decision.

It was a disappointment when I lost my seat, but it wasn't a surprise. You'd have had to have been a total Pollyanna to have thought that anything else was going to happen. All the pollsters told me, it was always the profile of a National seat. So I expected that to happen. And I'm fortunate that my husband's always been an absolute realist. I've never treated politics as anything but temporary. And that's one way of protecting yourself. And your family. Even if it takes up all of your time, it's still just a phase of your life.

Elizabeth Tennet

. . . you've got to have a thick skin.

I had been involved in the Labour Party extensively and I was working in Wellington. We had the Wellington Trades Council union group who used to meet regularly with the MPs. I had contacts with some of the women MPs. I knew Margaret Wilson quite well. I'd always held people like Helen Clark in very high regard, so it wasn't as though I'd come in from the sticks, never been to Parliament, that sort of thing.

I probably didn't have knowledge of the full extent of the hours of work. Or the total commitment to your life. But I had a reasonable idea about it, so I wasn't too shocked by it.

Since I've been an MP I've experienced the high point of 1987 where we seemed to be everybody's friend and then the low point in 1990 when nobody wanted to know you. There's a certain cynicism built in there, I suppose. I appreciate that how politicians and their political party are viewed is fairly dependent on the mood at any one time and that you shouldn't take anything personally

You are treated as a person based on how people feel about you and your party. When you're down, as I said, nobody wants to know you and they don't look at you in the street, they don't talk to you. Just goes with the territory.

It can be quite hurtful at times. In fact very hurtful. But you either bow out because you don't like it or you keep going because you've got higher goals you're trying to achieve. I think some politicians find that kind of pressure difficult. And also the personal pressure in their lives, and the fact that they're not willing to sacrifice any more of it. And I think women politicians are more prepared to bow out than men.

I felt very hurt over the 1990 defeat. But then I knew that it was coming a year before it came, so I was pretty well prepared for the election defeat on the night. But it's just very sad that all these things go on around you and most of it was caused by the Labour Party MPs themselves—the leadership fights and so on.

I guess for a first-term back-bencher it was a feeling of powerlessness to do anything about it. That made me angry. But then, you've got to have a thick skin.

Marie Hasler

All my energies go into thinking about what I am doing right now.

It takes a long time to unwind because you don't finish until ten-thirty at the earliest, unless you're in urgency. I don't get home till at least about midnight because often I work at my desk. I like to read, but I don't get the time to read the things I used to, like the *Times Literary Supplement* and the *Guardian Weekly*.

You haven't the time to get involved. I'm afraid novels are a thing of the past, which is a shame. So I'm choosy about what I read. I flip through the odd *Vogue* magazine, but that's an absolute luxury. I have to be very discriminating about the articles that I read.

I don't have long-term plans, because things change so much. I have absolutely no idea what I'll do after politics. There are a lot of things I could do, but I'll think about it when the time comes. At the moment all my energies go into thinking about what I'm doing right now. This is a difficult seat, but I've worked hard in the electorate and got to know people so it's going to be interesting to see how things develop.

Christine Fletcher

I'm trying to be everything to everybody.

Women still haven't made it in politics in the numbers that they should. And for those women who have made it, what have they compromised? I know in my party they look quite closely at me, I'm the only one down there with a young family where the partner hasn't sacrificed his career.

If you talk with Jenny Shipley or Ruth Richardson—any of those women—their partners are not working at the moment because they need a househusband, and I don't think you get two for the price of one. Until we wake up and recognize that, you're not going to get women selected as candidates, certainly not in safe seats. There are still big battles out there in political life. There are huge battles in commercial life. Most women I know are probably like me and are doing it at enormous expense to themselves.

My son was with a group of kids recently, and someone asked him what his mother did. He said, 'Oh, she just works.' I said, 'Why don't you tell them what I do?' He said, 'Hell no, mum. I wouldn't tell them that, it's too embarrassing.'

Most of the other parliamentarians come home on Friday night and say, 'I'm so stuffed I'm not going to be able to do anything.' When I come home my kids say, 'What's for dinner?' And I know I still have to go out and get the groceries for the week, I still have to go and deal with all those things that have to be dealt with.

I'm trying to be everything to everybody. That's why I probably can't sustain it more than two terms. There will be those who are watching who would hope that I fail in that time. Something has to give. We haven't won the war on child care yet, we haven't won the war in terms of divvying up the home life, all of those really corny things.

Judith Tizard

If you're in Opposition it's much more frustrating than being in Government.

I intend to try to get out when I'm fiftyish. My life is more or less divided into three. I started thinking seriously about politics in my late teens and it was fifteen years or so till I got into Parliament. I thought I'd spend fifteen years or so in Parliament and that would depend on elections and so forth. If you're in Opposition it's much more frustrating than being in Government. It will just depend on how things fall out. I'm not saying absolutely I'm going to resign at forty-nine, or retire, or whatever. But that would give me another fifteen years to do something until I'm sixty-five—to do something else that's different. My family is very long-lived. I expect at least another fifteen years after that driving everyone crazy being a bad-tempered old lady or something.

Margaret Moir

The first month I was up in Wellington I'd leave home on the Tuesday and get home on the Friday and sometimes realize I hadn't even phoned my husband all week.

It's not a healthy lifestyle, but I don't know how that or the workload could be improved. We do have people who help us full-time in the electorate, and we have people who help us full-time up in Wellington. I think partly we have to delegate more as MPs, but I am reluctant to do that because I think you start to lose a feel for what's going on if you delegate too much. I've been to a speed-reading course, that helps. But it's just a case of getting down to it, getting on with the important things like the electorate things and discarding a lot of the other stuff.

It's hard to keep up with friends, to actually take time out and even telephone them. The first month I was up in Wellington I'd leave home on the Tuesday and get home on the Friday and sometimes realize I hadn't even phoned my husband all week. I had to put a time in the diary to ring him, I really had to make a conscious effort to do that. It stunned me. He was somebody I'd lived with for so long and yet I hadn't actually spent five minutes ringing to say, 'Hi, how's things going?'

When I go to the supermarket, it takes me an hour to get around because people want to chat or they'll buttonhole me about something. My husband has just given up waiting. He says, 'You take the car and then you'll be in charge yourself.' I'm reasonably well-known here on the Coast, but I can be very anonymous elsewhere, which I find great.

That's one of the hardest things, losing that last little bit of privacy. As a local body politician I'd been used to being a public figure but half of my life was still private. I wasn't in the public eye all the time. Whereas now, even if I go to a football game or a church service or somebody's birthday party, I'm still the MP.

I'm no longer Margaret. It's something I quite treasured, that last little vestige of just being Margaret, just being able to slop around in a pair of dungarees or jeans and not worry. But I find I am concerned, I have to be tidy, even if I'm at a football game. People tend to expect you to be sort of reasonably dressed, and you're still on duty.

There are rewards, lots of them, but there are lots of drawbacks. It is very difficult to allocate special time for your family, even on a Sunday. I try to close Sundays off for my day at home, my day to choose what we'd like to do. But you're still in demand on the phone and your time isn't yours. So my advice would be to understand that the job becomes the most important thing and realize the commitment that you're making.

Joy McLauchlan

But even the Beehive—I wouldn't like to live there.

I spent six years around Parliament prior to my being elected, but it still didn't prepare me for the intensity of the job. It just governs every day. The incredible, long hours and the inability to have a social life.

You are constantly thinking about what's happening in politics and how this will be affected by whatever action you take. The feedback that you're getting, no matter where you are or whom you're talking to. You have to make a tremendous effort to say to people if you're with them, 'Look, I'm here as me today not as a politician or as a member of the Government.' I can see it from others' point of view. It's an opportunity for them to confront —and I use the word confront—any MP. But it also makes it very difficult for MPs to get away from that.

You lose contact with friends. I hope I haven't lost any of my old friends, but I certainly don't see them as often as I used to or as often as I would like to. In terms of friendships within Parliament, I have met people whom I believe I will have a lasting, lifelong friendship with. But there are others where we have come together for a purpose and there is no affinity other than politics.

I did have an idea of the kind of workload an MP takes on. I had been on a number of community commitees. I was a community representative on a number of organizations, so that part of the job was expected. There's a balancing act—because when you're in Opposition you can promise all sorts of things. It's lovely being in Opposition. You've got time to think, you've got time to postulate, people listen to you and think, 'Oh, yeah, that sounds reasonable.' But when you are in Government and you've got to balance the reality with the desirable; that's the emotionally hard bit.

Parliament buildings need refurbishing. It's not exactly a place you'd hold up to be a premier building of the nation, and it's not a particularly healthy building to live in and work in. Just the design and the air-conditioning and the furnishings and stuff. The thing is when we say we are going to refurbish the Beehive—which should have already been done, and I imagine will have to be done this decade—there's going to be a great outcry: 'Politicians are looking after themselves.' But there's not enough public recognition given to the seven or eight hundred people who actually work in that facility who need good working conditions. The

Joy McLauchlan, MP for Western Hutt, 1990–. Photos by Woolf, Wellington

parliamentarians who are there are quite small in number compared to them. Admittedly most of them work there by choice, and they could probably leave and work somewhere else. But at the end of the day it's their facilities, more so than the politicians who are in and out of the building.

I think back to the hue and cry over putting in the tunnel to link Bowen House and the Beehive. There were letters in the paper down here to the effect that we should all have an opportunity to run over our most unfavoured politicians. But when you think of the to-ing and fro-ing by the seven or eight hundred people—it's their building and it's totally unfair to subject them to less desirable working conditions because of a prejudice against politicians having good working conditions.

But even the Beehive—I wouldn't like to live there. Jim Bolger used to say quite seriously that when we were in Government in 1990 he would have liked to have stayed in the old building and put the Opposition in the Beehive. But, of course, in the old building there was a concern about Legionnaires' disease.

It's just the lifestyle. It's not easy to eat, regularly, good decent food. You're often rushing dinners, and lunch hours are usually meetings of one sort or another. We get maybe an hour at lunch-time and maybe two hours at dinner-time and invariably there will be meetings in those times. It's always a matter of rushing to put enough food in your system. And the long hours encourage me to eat, personally, far more chocolate than I know is good for me. There's not enough time for exercise. A number of Members make that an absolute priority and they go for their runs or their swims.

For me, every Sunday, or Saturday if it can't be Sunday, I go for an hour-and-a-half walk with a friend who also has a fairly pressured job. We walk very briskly with my little dog, talking about various aspects of work, but not politics. That's inappropriate, given her job is closely involved with politics, and mine. And I don't even know if she votes National and I wouldn't ask her. She's been a very long and good friend and we just go for this very brisk walk, talking about kids and friends and what's in the newspaper and what's happening. And that's a total switch off. It's good physical relaxation and intense effort, and also it's a good mental break as well.

I have excellent family support. My husband is committed to the National Party and works long volunteer hours for them. My children have always been supportive. I've always asked them before I've gone into each election, do you want me to go through this again, and how does it impact on your lives. They always say, 'No, go to it.' They have a very strong sense of everybody having to be involved to make things work. They're not too good at accepting people who criticize without actually getting stuck in and trying to do something about it.

I don't push them to be conservative. I've lived by that old maxim—because I'm proof of it myself—if you're not a socialist at twenty then you've got no heart, and if you're not a conservative at forty you've got no head. But I don't push them to follow my politics at all. We have very interesting discussions, as you can imagine.

At times you have to laugh or you'd cry. Stephanie is my electoral agent. She and I are both dark and have vaguely similar hairstyles, and she's had occasions where she's had people come in who've seen my photograph outside and they think she's me. And they're quite adamant that she's just pretending that she's not me.

And seeing the different facets of the human personality—you've got to be interested in people to do this job. You couldn't do it otherwise. And there are really some very interesting people around the place.

Some people who have a particular bee in their bonnet go around different electorates in the Hutt Valley. If they don't get satisfaction they try Paul [Swain], and if they don't get it from Paul they'll come here or go to Sonja [Davies] or whoever. Sonja and Paul are both Labour people but we do work quite regularly in the best interests of the Valley rather than from a strictly political sense. And the local folk really like that.

Sonja Davies

Too many memories.

I do some travelling but it's not generally Parliament that pays. Like I'm going to Yokohama to speak in four cities and the Japanese are paying for me to go. I went to India recently and Kathmandu and I paid for myself, but I can't do that often. I won't have all that much money when I retire.

My roots are in Nelson which is a beautiful place with wonderful people but I couldn't retire there. Too many memories around every corner. Too sad for me. Mark and Charlie. So I've got this cottage up in the Wairarapa. Out of Masterton. I'm making gardens. And if I don't want to travel over the hill I can catch the train. It's a wonderful train service. That's one thing that Nelson hasn't got. But they'd never try and get rid of it—there might be a revolution if they tried to get rid of the Wairarapa train. It's very well used and there's lots of commuters to Wellington, so it's pretty safe.

Fran Wilde

. . . most politicians crave a bit of ordinariness in their lives.

I was meant to go up to New York to speak at the United Nations. We hadn't had anyone in Central America for many years, so I called there on the way. The visit was part of a the big trade outreach to Latin America because there are big markets there— particularly Brazil and Argentina. Not Chile, I went there later when they got rid of Pinochet.

I picked up a bug somewhere, and the day I landed in Costa Rica it struck. It was terrible but I thought it was just a stomach bug. You get them all the time. Or I always seemed to get them. You just chuck up for a day and you stuff yourself full of pills and it goes away. Except it didn't stop. It went on and on.

They got the doctor who gave me an injection but it still went on. I was really ill and I said, 'Look I'm just going to have to go home. There's no point in continuing.' I was with Belinda, my private secretary, and the ambassador and his wife. In the end it was clear I wasn't going to get better there and the best thing to do was get back to New Zealand. So we crawled on to the plane and the plane crashed when we were taking off.

It was a Boeing 757—a big plane full of Americans. It's very hard to remember details of things like that because it all happened so quickly. I think we'd just fractionally lifted off. The wheels were off the ground. There was just a bang. We were at the front and I remember the hostess said, 'Oh, there's goes my hot coffee pot.' But it was more than just the coffee pot. We smashed back on to the ground. It went scrape, scrape, smash, smash along the ground. Everyone got down into the crash positon. I just thought, 'This is it. I'm going to die.'

The plane ground to a halt. They said, 'Out, everyone out.' The emergency chutes went down. We piled out and ran for our lives. But when she hit the ground, Belinda just stood there. I grabbed her and said, 'Come on.' I dragged her along because I thought the plane might blow up. It turned out she'd broken her foot when she hit the ground.

I was sick but I wasn't going to wait around to be blown up. The fuselage had broken in two. Thank God it wasn't Wellington. We would have crashed in the harbour. We got as far away as we could and everyone milled around. One passenger was having a heart attack. Eventually we got buses back to the hotel and I was still feeling really ill. We stayed another night and booked on a different airline. We took Belinda to the hospital where she had her foot put in plaster .

The saga went on and on. We landed in Los Angeles. I was exhausted and obviously not well. They had a wheelchair at the top of the plane door for Belinda. I was just about falling down and I half pushed her and half rode the wheelchair. We got into the baggage collection area. All the way through Latin America they'd given us bottles of rum. Everyone said, you must have a bottle of our special rum. I hate rum.

I dropped Belinda's bag and her bottle of rum broke. Well it stank. You can imagine—this pair of forlorn travellers with everybody milling around us. We got the mess cleaned up, then we went out through into the Air New Zealand check-in area. Because we'd left South America in a hurry and I had been too sick to pack properly I had tons of papers, particularly diplomatic and trade papers that you collect on these trips. My bag burst open and the contents went all over the floor—all these Foreign Affairs papers in the middle of Los Angeles airport. I was so sick I was almost falling over. However, we repacked and staggered onto the plane.

So I finally arrived home and went to the doctor. The bug still kept getting worse and they couldn't find out what it was. I'd lost a lot of weight by then—best diet I've ever been on. They put me into hospital and found out what it was. The doctor said, 'Oh don't worry, it only has a twenty per cent mortality rate in Latin America.'

Once they gave me the dope for it I was fine and I started getting better straight away. But when I went home I was still far from well. Then my legs and back started getting sore and my joints began swelling.

I thought, 'What's going on here?' All over, my whole body was swelling. I got somebody to take me up to the doctor, who informed me I had arthritis, triggered off by the bug. Every joint in my body, jawbone, the whole lot was affected by this reactive arthritis.

I couldn't walk. I was in a wheelchair. They gave me steroid injections in my joints, which was terrible. Very painful. But it worked and I started to get better. I went on to crutches and then on to a walking stick. I wasn't too good for a few months. At one stage I was very depressed, and I thought I was never going to walk again. I had no idea what might happen. There's a lot of ignorance about arthritis. It was pretty awful.

I was terrified of flying for ages after that, but I was Minister of Tourism so I had to fly. It's part of the job. But it was real white knuckle stuff for a couple of years. People think travel is one of the perks of office.

The institution of Parliament gobbles you up. You get absolutely removed from everyday life. It's not through choice—most politicians crave a bit of ordinariness in their lives.

Most MPs know what's going on, particularly the ones who represent poorer electorates. They hear about it every week, and they have an enormous amount of human misery presenting in their electorate clinics. But in a sense you have to learn how to cope with that and not get too emotionally involved, otherwise you'd go under. So the very act of coping means you're removing yourself from it.

You tend to get a smaller and smaller group of friends—that certainly happened to me. In the end you only go out socially with people who aren't going to hassle you all the time about what your party's doing, and aren't going to get into you about what you are and aren't doing.

So you go out with people who let you be, where you can just have an ordinary talk about anything at all, rather than politics.

People come up and abuse you on the street. I've been abused all over the place—particularly because of homosexual law reform. There's also been a lot of good things. People come up and say, 'You don't know me, but I just want to thank you for that.' Or else it may not even be the gay bill, or the adoption bill. Someone'll say, 'You helped me once', and you won't even remember who they are.

But to a lot of people a politician is just a politician. We're almost interchangeable. When I've been campaigning I've had someone confuse me with my opponent and come up and start abusing Fran Wilde to my face. And once I was walking near my house and someone walked past and said, 'I know you, don't I? You're Ruth Richardson.'

We're politicians. We're seen as being all the same. We're all as nasty as each other. It's pretty tough. All of us have suffered from that. It's not very nice that some people hate you. It's awful in fact.

4

THE MULDOON YEARS

Sir Robert Muldoon was a symbol of the old, male-dominated world of politics. He controlled New Zealand politics for long periods in the seventies and eighties. In his farewell speech he acknowledged his difficulty in coming to grips with the phenomenon of women in the House.

Several MPs gave Muldoon's politics as a reason why they first decided to become involved in politics. Others in his own party suggested that a big step towards independence was being able to look into his eyes and not turn away. Ironically, his first major defeat came about partly through the refusal of a young, gay feminist to bend her principles.

Marilyn Waring

I screamed and yelled and made a great deal of noise.

Your colleagues would try and break you however they could. There was no quarter given. If they thought that, spiritually and emotionally, they could crack you in Caucus or on the floor of the House, that your credibility would be broken, they'd try. But within those confines I could cross the floor. If I could stand it and I could make it across there was nothing to stop me. I didn't have rule 242 like the Labour women had.

I found the Springbok tour a very rough time. There were death threats after the Waikato game and I had the Police D-Squad protecting me. There was the incident of the 'frogmarch'. It was the debate in the House on the Springbok tour and at this particular time neither Muldoon nor Talboys was in the country. I left the House to go to my room because it was getting very tough.

I went to my room and as the division was coming I was 'assisted'(?) 'escorted'(?)—I guess these are euphemisms—by two colleagues, one on each arm, into the lobby. I screamed and yelled and made a great deal of noise. It was a very, very tough period for me.

When I finally left Parliament, it was like 'what a way to go'.[1] To go like that is not an opportunity that's offered to everybody. But then it's not one that most people would take either, since it costs you your superannuation.

Muldoon and I were locked in a room for two-and-a-half hours together

Dorothy Jelicich, MP for Hamilton West, 1972–75, at the swearing-in of the new Parliament, 1973. She is flanked by Stan (later Sir Stanley) Whitehead (Speaker), Norman King (MP for Birkenhead), Rt. Hon. Norman Kirk (Prime Minister), and William Laney (MP for Oamaru).

and when he left that room he then called the Caucus together, and then called the snap election. For the two-and-a-half hours that we were locked in there, Sue Wood was there; Don McKinnon was; Barrie Leay was there. This will be a story for me to tell one day. The entire effort was to get me to withdraw by any means possible. Pushing people in my face. Pushing the electorate in my face. Any way they could try and work it. But I knew from Muldoon's opening words, the moment I walked into that room, that he wasn't interested in my apologizing and withdrawing. Not at all. But the others were desperate for it. Muldoon drank heavily throughout the whole meeting—brandy and ginger. I drank orange juice.

The reason Caucus voted to go with the snap election that night was because the tide was going out so fast that some of them believed they might still hold their marginal seats in a July situation when they wouldn't hold them in November. I wasn't in the Caucus, but I had a verbatim report of the meeting from a colleague. Interesting enough, one or two people of principle—Richardson, for example, was among them—said, 'This Government has lost the confidence of the majority. That's why we will have elections.' She stayed with the constitutional principles, but she was one of the only people in the Caucus who did. Most of them wanted it because they might not lose quite so heavily.

My worst experience, cumulatively, must have been Tuesday mornings.[2] In the last year I cried on the aeroplane every Tuesday morning when I had to go to Wellington. The cumulative despair after being there for nine years—nothing compares to that.

Katherine O'Regan

He just couldn't understand women, how they thought.

I have never really experienced sexism, not blatant sexism where I felt as if I'd been absolutely cut out or ignored. Maybe there is some problem and I haven't noticed it. Some women have experienced dreadful discrimination. Yet Sir Robert Muldoon was always supportive of Marilyn Waring, certainly during the period of '78 when things were not good for her publicity-wise, and she came out.

He advised her to bite the dust and not put her head up until the dust was gone, just continue working. He was supportive of her, although he couldn't understand her. I don't think he ever understood women very well. He didn't realize that women can actually have other interests apart from home and children. He was of the old school. He just couldn't understand women, how they thought. Mind you very few men ever do understand women. It's a mystery I suppose. I did see the discrimination that Marilyn suffered.

Helen Clark

Nuclear-free was one of those genuinely community-based things that people can have a strong view on. A lot of those people were women.

Marilyn Waring's life must have been unspeakably awful. I was on perfectly amicable terms with her. She'd been to my home. She represented the area that I grew up in, and my father had been on her selection committee and had been a great advocate of hers.

The Prebble bill was what brought down the Government in the end, because with Marilyn Waring's defection Muldoon couldn't guarantee a Government majority on the issue. And Labour's promise to make New Zealand nuclear-free obviously then became a major issue in the '84 elections, and had to be acted on. Nuclear-free was one of those genuinely community-based things that people can have a strong view on. A lot of those people were women. Conference was consistently strong on the issues. People like Ann Hercus took an interest and made speeches about it. Bill Rowling took up the cause, although with that older generation of Labour politicians they still were part of that postwar settlement and support for ANZUS. To that extent, we went into the election with the policy of, 'Yes, we're nuclear-free but we want to stay in ANZUS'. That's become totally irrelevant now.

The Government would have fallen apart, anyway, on economic issues. By July '84 Muldoon had run out of every option for running the economy. He'd systematically closed them all off. In '82 he froze the economy, he froze wages, interest rates, dividend payments, everything was frozen. He really couldn't think of what else to do—someone had to break the mould. Marilyn Waring's action precipitated the election five months early, but I think they would have lost anyway.

Lianne Dalziel

. . . Muldoon and the unions politicized me more than anything else.

I developed an enormous, almost hatred towards Muldoon because of the '81 tour. The Springbok tour was just awful. I have very vivid memories of sort of going on protest marches, seeing policemen with visors and batons and riot shields. I wasn't particularly politically focused in my teens. So Muldoon and the unions politicized me more than anything else.

Anne Collins

He said that the Labour women MPs in '84 were so stroppy and so radical they wouldn't even let you open the door of Parliament for them.

The first day was just amazing. I think I was a bit awestruck. And all you had to do was just be sworn in. Then you came up to the front and swore or affirmed on the Bible. As I walked past the front bench of the Opposition there was a bit of a commotion. I didn't really know what had happened but Trevor Mallard told me later the comments were fairly sort of judgemental. Comments like, 'Aw, she's all right', and all that sort of schoolboy stuff.

I couldn't believe it, because it was my first day there. It was a bit like

Lianne Dalziel, MP for Christchurch Central, 1990–, as Secretary of the Canterbury Hotel Workers' Union, 1988.

being in church. Other people got very angry on my behalf. So I mentioned this in my maiden speech, that I was amazed that in this place of all places a woman couldn't walk past a group of blokes without being judged and commented on.

We'd been told not to be controversial in our maiden speeches because people listen politely and don't interrupt. I think I was a bit näive to say things like that and expect people to not react. They didn't, they sat through the speech, but Sir Robert Muldoon took a point of order against me.

The next thing I knew I was being interviewed on Australian radio. It was a bit of a shock that I got so much attention. I was taken off on *More Issues* and they had me very prim and proper saying, 'That's sexist, that's sexist'; but it was very funny, and it did draw attention to that sort of stuff.

The comments continued the whole time I was in Parliament. We eventually had a bit of a campaign, an organized strategy against it, because it got pretty nasty, not against me but against some of the other women. I can remember being rung up in the first month of being an MP by Radio Pacific, who'd had Muldoon on a Sunday show. He said that the Labour women MPs in '84 were so stroppy and so radical they wouldn't even let you open the door of Parliament for them.

Sir Robert always used to make comments to Fran Wilde and Annette, insinuating some sort of relationship there. Others of them made comments about our sex life in general.

Annette King's mother had been very sick and she'd been staying with Annette. She'd been in hospital and been having treatment here in the hospital, and Annette was so worried about her that she put her into her own bed and slept on a mattress on the floor. So that if anything happened in the night she would be there. With Parliament sitting late and her mother's illness and everything she was very tired.

This one morning she came in and the first comment that greeted her was, 'Do you remember whose bed you slept in last night?' That was so unfair and so nasty, and it just wouldn't have been said to a man. Margaret Austin took a point of order and said it was sexual harrassment. It caused quite a fuss. That's why I ended up being interviewed. And I had pieces of Hansard that I could actually read out on Paul Holmes's show.

After that programme it seemed that a lot of complaints went into the National Party. A lot of their women were very upset at the way the MPs were behaving. And it did seem to calm down after that. But the feelings against women MPs were always just below the surface, it didn't need much to bring them out.

Jenny Shipley

There was an unspoken club of people in Caucus who had looked Sir Robert Muldoon in the eye and had argued the point against him and survived.

I made a valedictory when Muldoon left and acknowledged that he had been very hard on women in his life and had made it harder for some women, including myself, to be in politics. But, for all that, he needed acknowledgement for the fact that some of the most radical legislation that protects women was passed while he was Prime Minister. I don't think that can slip by without notice.

And I also told a story of a breakfast or lunch, I can't recall which, that I had had with him. This was not terribly long before he announced his retirement. He was in a more conciliatory mood than often and he said, well he wasn't sure what we women brought to Parliament but he would have to concede that it was for the better. And that is the only time he ever got near to acknowledging that we had a contribution to make.

What he couldn't cope with was people who would not simply give in to him. And there was an unspoken club of people in Caucus who had looked Sir Robert Muldoon in the eye and had argued the point against him and survived. And it's not an accident that some of the women crossed that hurdle very early.

As he lost the grip of being able to frighten the stuffing out of people, I think his sadness increased. He thought that because he held a view, that others would give in. And of course there were some very big issues that he and I had to argue through, even towards the very last part of his time in Parliament, not the least of which was superannuation.

He just didn't have credible arguments on the analysis, and in this day and age it's not good enough to just try and frighten people into submission, or to dominate. You've got to be able to put a case on its merits.

Annette King

He was a really difficult old bugger, but he was fascinating . . .

I'm one of those people who were fascinated by Muldoon. I hated the things he did to New Zealand—his economic policy and the total control that he had over the country. He was a powerful person. But on a personal level I found him really fascinating, and I discovered a real sense of humour beneath a very gruff exterior, which scared a lot of people. I got to quite like him. We used to spend quite a long time talking together. He was a really difficult old bugger, but he was fascinating and there was something likeable about him.

I think a sense of humour in a politician is a real attribute. You've got to have a sense of humour. I think a lot of people never saw Muldoon's sense of humour. It was very hard for him to be funny. They often don't expect politicians to be funny.

Fran Wilde

He was an old-fashioned man who thought women should be in the kitchen or in the bed.

There's always been a bit of sexism around; as incidents arose we just tried to deal with them. The women always took a strong stand. It was important that we were able to work as a group. We may have had differences on some issues but on a lot of core women's issues we were united.

We were very vigilant about things like sexist language, not just in the House but in people's speeches. We used to keep an eye out on our colleagues and tell them when we thought they were being offensive. Some of them hadn't thought anything about it; but women would blanch when they heard sexist jokes.

We weren't being ideological terrorists. We were just saying, 'Hey guys, it's not actually very appropriate to tell those sorts of jokes now.' They reflected attitudes that were not acceptable in policy makers.

It was a lot worse when I first got into Parliament. For example, if a group of women MPs happened to be sitting together anywhere, the men would always comment on it. Because there were so few women around it was an unusual sight. That wouldn't happen now. The institution has moved a lot.

One thing I remember happened to me. I was speaking on a foreign policy issue and I mentioned the United States. At that stage I was going out with an American who lived in Wellington and the parliamentarians knew that because they'd seen me with him. One of their male MPs yelled out, 'Tell us about your American friend, what's he like in bed?' I thought, 'I'm not hearing this, I'll just ignore it', and I kept speaking. But he yelled it out again.

The best thing for me to have done would have been to stop and get it in Hansard because that would have exposed him. I chose to ignore it, but I was very angry. It was the pits. All of our lot were pretty mad. One of my female colleagues was Anne Collins (then Fraser). She was the Member for the neighbouring electorate and she went to see this MP the next day.

Only Anne could say this. She told him she'd had a call from his local women's network and they wanted to publish the comment in their newsletter. Of course there was no such thing. But this guy freaked out and backed off completely. The thought of his being pilloried by a women's network was too much for him.

Muldoon did it to me once. Annette King and I were sitting together one night and we chipped him about something. He said, 'If you don't stop that I'll tell the House who you're sleeping with at the moment.' Can you imagine that from the great elder statesman of New Zealand?

Muldoon was a classic. He was an old-fashioned guy who thought women should be in the kitchen or in the bed. He just couldn't cope with women who were upfront. Any woman who was prepared to have him on and who gave as good as she got, he found that very difficult.

So it could be pretty nasty, but maybe that's how New Zealand society was then. Other places in society would have been worse than this; some would have been better. It's a House of Representatives, I suppose.

Marie Hasler

. . . he made politics quite exciting . . .

When it comes to role models I don't think I consciously had anyone. There were some politicians whom I admired. In a funny way Sir Robert Muldoon had a lot of effect on me because he made politics quite exciting, especially conservative politics which had been quite dull. Until he came along they had been mostly rural members and more conservative. I certainly didn't agree with everything he did, but in the early days he was a breath of fresh air.

He was sometimes sexist but he knew that he was. He'd been brought up by his mother and I think he admired women tremendously. That was the problem, he put them on a pedestal. He once said to me he couldn't really bring himself to be nasty to a woman, and he did have a fairly aggressive style in politics. He didn't find it easy to treat them as he would a male politician. He was a victim of his own upbringing and he was quite honest about it.

Notes
1. In June 1984, in the face of the Government's insistence that she vote against the Opposition's 'nuclear-free' bill, Marilyn Waring decided to resign from the National Caucus and declare herself an independent Member. This action has been regarded as instrumental in prompting Sir Robert Muldoon's decision to call a snap election. Ms Waring did not subsequently seek re-election to Parliament.
2. When in session, the House usually sits on Tuesday mornings and rises on Thursday evenings.

5

LANGE AND DOUGLAS

Perhaps the most significant challenge to New Zealand's political complacency this century came from the Labour Government of 1984–90. The complex internal dynamic of this administration may perhaps be typified by the contrast between Prime Minister David Lange's championing of New Zealand's nuclear-free status on one hand and finance minister Roger Douglas's encouragement of radical, free-market economic policies on the other.

For MPs who joined the Labour Party with ideals of improving social conditions it was not an easy time. Significantly, when the tide turned against Rogernomics, women played a central role in the ensuing action.

Helen Clark

. . . what could you talk to Roger about?

By the night of the 1984 election we certainly expected to win. It was a time of mixed feelings, to be frank. One knew that a Government led by Lange with Douglas pulling the strings was probably going to have its problems. I have enormous ambivalence about that. Of course you want to win, but the chances were it was going to fly apart, and it did.

You really didn't have anything in common with Roger. I think that was the problem with the first three years I was there: that there were very few people you actually had anything in common with. The '84 victory brought in a lot of people not dissimilar to oneself in terms of education and background. But, yeah, what could you talk to Roger about?

When a party goes into Government after a long time in Opposition, the people who go into Cabinet tend to be the ones who have been there longest in Opposition. And that happened. I guess you could say there was quite an age and perception gap between those in and those out.

You could write a number of books about what went wrong with the Fourth Labour Government. What went wrong was it didn't have a clear economic agenda when it took up power. Douglas supplied one. The key group of ministers from the Prime Minister, Deputy Prime Minister, and his associates embraced it. They shoved it down everybody's throats.

Most of the Caucus sort of fell into line thinking, 'Oh well, we've got a big mandate and, yes, you've got to have new ways' and so on.

What makes me a little bit cynical six or seven years down the track is people saying Labour departed from its principles. It did, but no one was saying that in 1987 when the major departure from principle had occurred and some of us had been ostracized for opposing it. But so long as the bubble sort of stayed up in the air people were endorsing it. And the bitterness only came when the inevitable happened and the bubble burst with the sharemarket crash. It wasn't the second three years when Labour went off the rails of traditional principles, it was the first three that laid the basis for it.

I have sort of become a voice for change in the whole way in which Budgets are drawn up, because I think it's disgraceful. The Budget is drawn up in the secrecy of the Cabinet. There's no consultation. On the night that the Budget is read to Parliament at seven-thirty, the Caucus has got it at half-past-six or something like that, and is told what is in it. So we were brought together in 1984 and told about GST and all those big decisions.

There was no consultation on the critical decisions that flowed through the second part of '84: fast, radical changes on tariffs, economic deregulation, banking deregulation, floating the currency, GST. The move to indirect taxation and in family support which cut across the old universal support ideas. None of those decisions were taken with involvement of MPs outside the Cabinet.

The people who were driving it were very bright and very able, and they conscripted some of the others. I think there were always voices like Russell Marshall's which said, 'Hang on, this wasn't what we were put here to do.' They were regarded as totally irrelevant. All this is the background to where Parliament's ended up today: in complete odium in the public mind. Absolutely outrageous.

While one can criticize Muldoon in many ways, Muldoon was a very shrewd judge of what the public would accept. But I think the way Douglas and Co. acted was to take the view that they knew best. They didn't have to consult with anyone. Things had to be done, you couldn't wait. I think that's where the whole thing went off the rails.

The initial rush after deregulation was the bubble. New companies arose out of it. A lot of people bought shares who had never owned shares before and there was all sorts of excitement. Then the bubble burst, and when the crash came it stripped away the chimera of prosperity. There was no prosperity. There'd been a kind of rush of activity, but the bubble burst and it all went. But we never had any chance to debate that. There was never any alternative put up. It was just that the Caucus was told what was happening.

There used to be a group of around twelve MPs who met to try and focus

some opposition to all of this. I was part of it. Jim Anderton and Fran Wilde
were in it. We discussed the Budget in 1984 after it was presented, and it
was decided that I would lead off with an attack on it in the Caucus, which I
did. The group was ignored. And that's just the way it played.

The problem with the '87 election was the slogan, 'It's time to finish the
job.' There were two completely different ideas about what that meant. The
Centre-Left of the party said, 'Let's get on with the economic and social
half.' David Lange genuinely believed that.

But Roger Douglas said, 'No, let's deregulate that as well.' Straight after
the '87 election he put up to the Cabinet Policy Committee the proposal to
sell Petrocorp which clearly, in retrospect, was the first of the privatizations.

We had sold corporatization on the basis that it made State entre-
preneurial activities more efficient. The difference between us and the
National Party was that we wouldn't privatize. It was believed that you could
have effective and enterprising State companies which put a return to the
taxpayer.

I remember naïvely going off to that Cabinet committee and saying,
'Look, there's a whole lot of reasons why this shouldn't be done.' Roger
Douglas got quite agitated saying, 'What the hell is she on about?'

I was right outside the paradigm, and they couldn't have given a stuff
about what the public thought or what the Caucus thought. It was just
railroaded through. And I'm sure this is what happened with the first three
years. The way Douglas operated with the Cabinet was simply to dump
major proposals on the table in the morning that no one had the time to read.
Often, not even at the start of the meeting just sometime during the meeting,
they'd come in with a major proposal they wanted a decision on. And the
opposition to it was too weak to stop it.

No wonder people started to feel disempowered—we were all totally
disempowered. It was incredibly distressing. I suppose the thing that really
bugs me most about the last couple of years was that most of the cheer group
for Rogernomics left Parliament and the rest of us had to pick up all the
odium of things that we never wanted to do in the first place. Someone said
to me, 'That's management, you have to take responsibility.'

When I came into the Cabinet in 1987, the threat to our social policy from
the Right was far worse than I had imagined. I popped in to see one minister
who said, 'I know you're going to get Housing. It will have to become an
SOE but that's fine.'

I thought, 'Hang on a minute, that's not fine at all.' I have no doubt that I
was appointed Minister of Housing because David Lange saw me as a block
to the New Right approach. The first thing that happened was that I got all
the briefing papers. I remember I went away to Surfers' Paradise for about

six days after the election. I had some sleep and read the briefing papers.

I was just appalled at what I read. What Luxton and the Nats have now done to the Housing Corporation was what was on the agenda when I became Minister of Housing in July '87. The entire time that Douglas was there I was fighting that. I stopped it, but it took some work.

Douglas tried to rush it with the December 1987 economic package. He put up a proposal to the Cabinet with that package which was that State housing was to go in total. Three-quarters of the houses were to be sold on the open market and the other quarter were to be given to the social service agencies which were dealing with people that Treasury deemed to be hopeless cases—schizophrenics, battered women, and so on. So they'd be handed over on a one-off basis to them and that would quit the State's obligation. And of course all the loan portfolio would go and all the rest of it.

I was beside myself with rage. I remember somewhere in the Minister of Finance's great detailed annexes reading: 'What would be the role of ministers? Their role will be to announce these proposals'! Absolutely preposterous. Someday someone will write the full book about it

The Cabinet was pretty shocked at what it saw. In the end they accepted a modified version of the package, although there were still obviously problems with that. But as far as we knew, this nonsense about what was to happen to Housing had been discarded.

It was just before Christmas, and I went away for a couple of weeks' holiday. When I got back I rang senior Housing officials just to see what had been happening while I'd been away. I found that Roger Douglas, in everyone's absence, had had Treasury, Housing, and everyone else working on implementation of the original plans that he'd put to the Cabinet.

I mean, I was the Minister of Housing; I came back and rang Housing officials and said, 'What have you been doing?' They said, 'We've been working with Treasury on these proposals arising out of the economic package.' I got them to fax up what they were working on. Bloody hell, it was all this original stuff.

I went home and read them. I went round to a friend's place for a function at the weekend and she said, 'You don't look very well, what's wrong?' And I just burst into tears, and said, 'You have no idea what they're trying to do.'

I'd made up my mind that, if those housing proposals were accepted, that I was going then. I could not stay as Minister of Housing. Then I'd thought we'd got rid of them. It was just outrageous.

So I got on a plane and went down to Wellington to see Lange and I said: 'Look, I don't know what's been going on while I've been away, but I didn't become Minister of Housing to preside over the demolition of State housing and public housing policy. But what's happened?'

Of course David Lange had spent the whole Christmas break sitting in his office coming to grips with what the Minister of Finance's real agenda was. Like rust, Roger and the Treasury never slept. They were moving to implement things that hadn't been agreed to. It was shortly after that, of course, that the Prime Minister went to the press conference and said it was time for a cup of tea. Roger Douglas flew back from London and then it was all on. It was a slow drama that played out over the course of a year.

As far as anyone knew, Roger Douglas's economic package was about cutting tax rates. Never anything about housing, never anything about health. What he was not open about with the Cabinet was that the figures he put up justifying the loss in tax rates were not sustainable without a significant decline in State provision.

I think he misled the Cabinet. He was relying on huge cuts in social services to finance it. What would have happened three months down the track? I assume he would have come in and said, 'The fiscal position's much worse than we think. The taxes are lower, we can't put them back up again', and it would have been a repeat of the original December package.

The problem through that whole period, right through to Roger Douglas finally going, was that most of the Cabinet and the Caucus thought that it was a personality clash, that David and Roger would sit down and have a drink together and talk it through and it would be all right. But that was impossible. It was a deep philosophical division. The only criticism you can make of David Lange is that he let it run so long and so far. The crisis of conscience shouldn't have come in April '87, and then in January. It should have come years before.

What I hadn't known, of course, was that in April 1987 Douglas had put proposals like that up to David Lange. He wanted to go before the election with all this New Right, individual choice, you pay less tax, and be able to choose the education you want for your children, and purchase it directly yourself. Who needs the State making these decisions? What's the State got to do with education? What's the State got to do with housing? This is an affordability problem. People will get vouchers.

He tried all that in April '87 and they told him to go away. Then he came back and back and back. It was pretty obvious to me by then that his staying was just not compatible with being a Labour Government.

We were dealing with people who were prepared to lose elections rather than be proved wrong. Of course, after the Minister of Finance stepped down, he went after the Prime Minister. It was sort of like the slow hunting of an animal. In the end it's sustained so much damage it's got to go. They pulled the whole show down with it.

They had a lot of strength in our Caucus, that was the problem. I mean

Sonja Davies, MP for Pencarrow, 1987–, and Rt. Hon. Helen Clark.

the whole thing would never have run so far if it hadn't been that the majority of people went along with it.

I think people like Margaret Shields were in an incredibly difficult position. She was more or less where Russell Marshall was in the Cabinet, but she was marginalized, and that was very hard. If you looked at the women in the Caucus, some were in marginal seats and they got a bit swept along with the excitement. They'd never been in Parliament before. Roger worked very hard on the Caucus. He was very good to a number of the marginal seat members, which helped their campaign funding in 1987.

So you wouldn't have got a common view on it. There were quite sharp divisions, and the Women's Caucus really didn't talk about those issues. It talked more about the things it could influence like child-care and domestic violence.

In the first three years of the Government, after the debacle of the '84 budget and knowing that you didn't have any say at all, I buried myself in foreign affairs work. For the three years I travelled a great deal. I would have been out of the country six or seven times a year.

What was in my mind was that if what happened to me in '84—being excluded from the club—had happened in '87, I would then leave in 1990. Because I didn't go into Parliament to sort of sit around in Opposition in Government. If things hadn't changed in '87 I would have gone. In '87 I did get enough support to go into the Cabinet because there were sufficient retirements. Then I took the view that you did what you could.

I certainly worked very hard to protect housing, and I quite enjoyed the conservation job. Then when the great fallout came I got the chance to do health. That was a big opportunity. Then when I became Minister of Labour, Stan Rodger had actually done a very good job protecting the labour market from deregulation. So that wasn't highly vulnerable under the Labour Government and there were other things to do there. I've always been fairly contemptuous of people like Anderton who just walked away from it, because clearly in two-party politics the Labour Party was the only vehicle that there was if you had any interest in a social democratic agenda. If you walked away, you were effectively saying, 'It's not worth fighting for.'

Jenny Kirk

. . . in fact, in Parliament, because you were a woman,
you were not listened to. . .

My expectations? I had expected, for instance, that the policy the Labour Party put out would be the policy that I would be helping to put into place. Labour had dealt, or so they said, with the economic changes. The term that I went in was going to deal with the social changes.

I had looked at the Labour women's policy and I had agreed with that, and I had looked at the social policy and I had agreed with that. Otherwise I would not have stood. I believed that Labour was a party that stood for equality for people and positive action on social issues. We had some specific policies for improving the lifestyle of women and children. Then I went in and found that those policies were constantly undermined by the Government's economic policy, which was totally at odds with the social aspirations of Labour people, whom I represented.

I had realized there was something going on, but I had thought that those people who were putting policy into place would listen to reason—they would listen to the experiences of people who had actual experience of living under those sorts of conditions. And that they would be prepared to compromise. That didn't happen. I didn't expect to go in and have a constant battle for three years, but that is what happened.

I expected people would work together within Labour, because Labour had a reputation of being an organization that believed in collective decision-making and consensus, and that didn't happen either. In Caucus you got harangued.

I had expected that Labour politicians would listen to Labour women because Labour also had this reputation of being an equality party, and they said things that indicated that. But in fact in Parliament, because you were a woman, you were not listened to—that is, if you were dealing with a single issue. If you did something on a *collective* basis you had more chance of being listened to.

Gender deafness, yes that's what it was. I also expected to be treated like an adult, but the parliamentary institution does not treat its members like adults. I think most of the back-bench MPs felt this frustration. Thousands of women believed in Labour's social policy and Labour lost a lot of women's votes, because, although we were implementing women's policies, these were undermined by the economic policy.

When I found I wasn't being listened to I figured out ways of making those same comments and suggestions through friendly men, who were then listened to, so of course the suggestions were taken up. But I wasn't credited with the ideas, I think that's a strategy a lot of women in high places use. I got a bit irritated not being credited with the ideas, but it was more important to get the ideas taken up.

People in my situation in Government were opposed to the Government's economic direction and were trying to stop it. We wanted to see the social policy put in—particularly the women's policy, which in the end we did actually achieve. A significant 'lever' in getting legislative and political action on these issues was the poll results which showed we were losing the women's vote.

Sonja Davies

Roger Douglas says the only thing he regrets is not going faster and finishing.

Muldoon had an unerring instinct for knowing just how far he could push the public. He was a great person for saying, 'I'm going to do x, y, z.' And everybody went, 'Gasp, how terrible!' Then he'd bring it in just slightly softer, something not quite as hard as that. And people would say, 'Oh, yes, that's better, isn't it?' It's very clever, that. Roger Douglas simply didn't care, he was not interested.

Now, if you believe Roger, he's reworking the economies of Eastern Europe. We went and heard the new ambassador for the Confederation of Independent States in Russia. They were talking about economics and David Lange was sitting next to me. I said to him, 'I have a terrible sense of déjà vu.' And he said, 'It's very familiar.' Roger Douglas says the only thing he regrets is not going faster and finishing.

I don't believe in the trickle-down theory, I don't believe in the light at the end of the tunnel or the level playing field. I came in in '87 basically to try to turn the thing around, to deflect people away from Rogernomics because I could see what it was doing to people out there and what it was doing to the fabric of our lives.

For example, I went down to Hokitika and up to Gisborne on consecutive weekends, and they just happened to be the weekends when the State Services Commission representative had gone to both places to tell forestry people that they had the weekend to apply for their jobs and only a third of them would get them.

In both cases, the whole town was in shock. I met women with husbands who were in their early fifties who confidently expected to perhaps go up the ladder a bit more and finish their careers out in forestry—their lives were just completely shattered. They'd never had any experience of this.

I came back and I said that I believed that before we did anything like that we should have done an evaluation. We should have had a look to see what that action was going to do schools, to the hospitals, to the shops, to the community and, if they insisted on going ahead and doing it, devise ways of helping the people through that time. But I was told there wasn't time for that.

When it started we knew that if we went into Caucus on a Thursday morning that we were never going to win. There were just too many. It was pretty demoralizing. For the first six months in '87 we were way over there, in Siberia [the Lockwood block behind the Parliamentary Library]. I actually took over Jim Anderton's office. And they were in the Beehive, so it was east is east and west is west. You really only saw them if you were on a Caucus committee that their portfolio had an input into, or at Caucus. Or unless you wanted to take somebody to see them. But you never really sat down and talked.

But coming in was very hard, because of the whole Rogernomics thing which was an anathema to me. Some of the Women's Caucus believed in it and others just didn't want to get involved. People like Helen Clark were having their own battle—she and Margaret Shields had their real struggles. When Helen was wanting to bring in the Pay Equity legislation she had battles, not only with departmental people but with her own colleagues. But she did it and I think that's very important. I think we all got caught up in it. People say, 'You didn't stop it so you were part of it.'

Now it's quite different. It's good the way we're going, the fact that the party has realized now. We don't offer the public one single thing that we can't deliver. Better to offer nothing than offer things that you can't deliver.

Annette King

. . . they couldn't talk about what the real problem was,
they couldn't talk about their own feelings.

There were three back-benchers who were asked to try to mediate or find
out what the problem was between Lange and Douglas. Jim Sutton, Clive
Mathewson, and I were asked to be the liaison with the two of them, and we
had several meetings with them. Because no one could really understand
what the problem was. If Lange and Douglas were questioned they both
would tell you they had no problems with each other.

They were very amicable. They were both very pleasant to each other.
But in my view, in typical male fashion they couldn't talk about what the
real problem was, they couldn't talk about their own feelings.

On reflection it was probably the wrong way to go about it because they
were all men who had a macho approach to life. Without being critical of
Jim and Clive, because they were trying hard, they're not the sort of men
who would want to talk about feelings either—not in that forum. They might
have one to one. That may have been a mistake in the way we tried to do it.
It was kind of like a posse coming to extract information from you. They
didn't want to give it to you in that forum so it didn't really work.

In hindsight the philosophical differences were too deep, but at the time
people could only remember all the things that had been said before. Lange
and Douglas had been the Siamese twins. One was supporting the other and
the Cabinet solidarity had been there for everybody to see. And suddenly,
almost like a wave of a wand, it changed. None of us were in the Cabinet or
in the inner circle, so none of us knew what was going on. People didn't see
it as philosophical to start with. They thought there must have been
something that had gone on because it was so sudden.

Personally I disagreed with the New Right policies, but some changes had
to be made. Regardless of where they came from, I don't think there's
anybody in there who didn't agree that some changes had to be made.

One of the problems is you come into Parliament, like I did, where
you've got a political perspective but you've worked in a totally different
field. At that stage I'd never worked in the area of business or had any
business skills at all.

Take something like do you devalue or not? I wouldn't have known any
more about devaluing than most of New Zealand when it came to floating
the dollar. The decisons that were made—for many people like myself who
were back-benchers—what were the alternatives? What were arguments?

For most people you accepted the arguments that were put to you by your senior colleagues in the Cabinet. The arguments were very strong for changes from the sort of regime we had under Muldoon.

Where I think we went wrong is that we became hooked on change and the rhetoric of change. We as a Government believed what we were doing was absolutely right. Like some sort of vision that we had. And the links with the people who were giving you their feedback became less important as you became more convinced that you were doing the right thing. Some of it was right. Some of it I don't think we did right at all.

6

HOUSE WORK

The way the House of Representatives is run is the subject of almost uniform criticism and dissatisfaction. The rules and customs are so complicated that it can be years before MPs fully grasp them. Some MPs highlighted the fact that, often, the most effective weapon an Opposition can wield is its capacity for wasting time. In the electorate, too, demands are heavy. Calls for change are not new, but they are articulated here with considerable force.

Ruth Richardson

Women tend to get to the point more than the boys.

For three years I was a back-bench MP and for six years I was in Opposition. I became a front-bencher with senior responsibility, first in education and then in finance, but that is just kindergarten compared to the workload you've got as a senior Cabinet minister.

You've got the combination of tearing yourself three ways. One is your Cabinet responsibilities, the second is your constituent responsibilities, and the third, and certainly not least, is your family responsibilities. So the workload is very, very substantial. I am not a workaholic as such, but I've been sitting here today while the family's been out sailing for the day, and I've been working all day. And I'm liable to be working all night. I would start work on a typical day between 6 or 7 a.m. and I would work until midnight, typically.

I've got superb support staff, both in my electorate and in my ministerial office. So I've got the best organized, best focused, most supportive staff you could hope to have. It depends on the nature of your responsibility. Whether you're an activist or not. I've got one of those jobs where you have got a very big canvas. So it's not just a matter of knowing your own portfolios, I've got a responsibility to range over the field. So my particular job brings with it an extra workload.

Management of time is very important. Meetings tend to be very prolonged. I'd like to see a lot more women in Parliament because I think women are more economical with their use of time. That's engaging in some outrageous stereotyping, but I find it generally true. Women tend to get to the point more than the boys.

Hon. Ruth Richardson, MP for Selwyn, 1981–; Minister of Finance, 1990–.
Evening Post

As a Cabinet minister you have a different relationship to Parliament than if you are a back-bencher participating on select committees. I think Parliament paints itself far too much into an irrelevant or an ill-behaved corner. Lack of standards and lack of relevance in debate makes Parliament a bore and a chore for a Cabinet minister. I certainly didn't used to have that approach. I was an enthusiastic member of parliamentary select committees, I enjoyed debates. Increasingly, I find Parliament basically the last to reform itself.

But, in terms of actual time, I guess if you were a minister in the Keith Holyoake era when you didn't have debt, and when the country was cruising, and wealth was increasing, then that tended to be a far less demanding environment than it is now when there are many more issues to be tackled to secure results for New Zealanders and those that you serve.

So it's not an ideal situation but, inventive though many of us are, I cannot see an easy answer to the problem of extreme demands of time and pressure. My own personal answer is to try and pace myself and keep fit.

Sonja Davies

. . . I think the people who just want the [parliamentary] system to change for the sake of change are wrong in thinking that will bring integrity and justice.

There are good times. The times I like best are going out and talking to people, meeting groups, and of course our Women's Caucus. Mind you it's very hard to get it together, because there's always one of us speaking, or waiting to speak. So if we have groups up to meet us—there's sometimes two or three—the people can feel a bit put out that we're not giving them sufficient importance: but it's not that, it's that if you're down to speak, you're down to speak.

But we always have afternoon tea and we get along fine. It's an oasis. I think that's great, and that's the strength of it. That's why I feel sorry for people like Marilyn who didn't have other like-minded women. She was a lonely voice in here. She's now very strong. She's very special.

I think Parliament will change because the people want it to change. But I think the people who just want the system to change for the sake of change are wrong in thinking that will bring integrity and justice. It needs more than that.

Jenny Shipley

. . . there is a thread that binds us.

I think women run things differently. I'm sure if you did a survey of ministerial offices mine would be one of the more unusual ones there. Simply because that's how I like to function. And there's a reasonably high degree of hilarity.

When I hire people I hire them for their personality and their skills, and we have an unusual office in every respect. But they are very creative people and they are one hundred per cent reliable. I don't ask my people when I employ them what their politics are, unlike some of my colleagues. It's a very close office. We go out to dinner reasonably regularly as a group. Not as a staff dinner, but because every now and then we think it's a good idea.

*Hon. Jenny Shipley, MP for Ashburton, 1987–; Minister of Social Welfare,
Minister of Women's Affairs, 1990–.*

There isn't, shall we say, a hierarchical structure. There is no gross
familiarity either, it's simply that there's a job to be done. I rely on these
people and trust them to actually keep not only my personal interests
reasonably well focused, but also get on with the job and get the stuff done.
There are days when it gets terrible, because our office has been under huge
pressure in the last eighteen months. We've had to have personal management systems to survive. But, for all that, I think around the building people
perceive that our office is one of the better managed.

The women in the House are a very diverse group. You could split them a
number of ways, not the least of which would be the party lines way. There's
the materialistic approach to feminism where we speak on behalf of all
women and women want this or women want that. There's one group that
thinks that. And there's one group which thinks that this approach is simply

outdated and the new wave of feminism requires us to have a fair framework, where you've got points of appeal, but that people get on with their lives and deal with issues of equity in a managed sense, not in a sort of collective, hold hands and pray sense.

So there are different views, as I say. But at the end of the day, there is a thread that binds us.

Ruth Richardson and I and Katherine O'Regan were the only National women Members prior to the election, and we met regularly at that time, on a relatively informal basis. To call it a Caucus is an unnecessary formality and, you know, the New Zealand committee syndrome. But certainly now that we've got eight women there, we do have a regular Caucus. It's important to get the eight women together. Not all of them attend all the time. It's a strong group but, now that we're in Government, Ruth or I or Katherine try to be there as often as we can. It's not easy to be there as regularly as one would hope. But it certainly is very active.

Anne Collins

There's a hell of a lot of time wasted.

Select committees, Caucus meetings, party conferences—that's where it really happens. The House is just a debating chamber. It's meant to be where the public has access to everybody's views, but that's all it is really. There's a hell of a lot of time wasted.

You're so driven by the amount of work that goes through. I think the Labour Party, if it got back into Government, would set itself a more reasonable agenda. We reformed everything there was to reform. There wasn't a portfolio left untouched. That's typical of a Labour Government, because you think you're only there for three years. It's what we normally get given, and so we go like bats out of hell. When we got six years we couldn't believe our luck and sped it up instead of slowing it down.

So I think we're being more realistic next time. But there are some things like the Budget debate; we did cut down the hours with that. It's got more sensible since Geoffrey Palmer.

My advice to anyone thinking of taking up that life is simple. That your friends and family will always be the most important. You'll think that the demands of the job and the demands of the constituents are overwhelmingly important at the time. But in the long run they're probably not as important as people make you believe.

A lot of the time that you spend with individual constituents can just as efficiently and just as effectively be dealt with by your electorate secretary. If you're a constituent, you ring up on a Tuesday and you wait till the weekend to see the MP. A good electorate secretary could probably sort it out by the time the MP got home. Unless it's something you've got to take to a minister or something like that. And it can be done on the phone. I was lucky in that I had an excellent electorate secretary who really worked hard with the government departments.

Probably the atmosphere is different now. If you went to Social Welfare when we were in Government you'd always get something. Now people want to see their MP because it seems that people can't solve their problems. You're just told to go to foodbanks or Community Advice Bureaux. So that might be a different sort of role. I wouldn't mind being an electorate secretary. It's a job that I could do. And you're home at night.

Helen Clark

We used to have ridiculous committees.

When I first went in it was hard, no question about that. I mean you weren't part of the club—not part of where it really happens. I wanted to go on the Foreign Affairs Committee because I was always interested in that. I did go on as junior Opposition Member. We used to have ridiculous committees. There'd be a one-hour hearing, and you'd be lucky to get your question in at the end at all. So that wasn't terrifically satisfying.

The Foreign Affairs Committee was totally unsatisfactory. I made a lot of changes when I became chair. Geoffrey Palmer, of course, reformed the select committee structure so you could do more with it.

The other committee I was allocated to was Statutes Revision and I found that just appallingly tedious. After about a year I went to Jonathan Hunt and said I just didn't want to be on it any more. I had better things to do with my time. It was the sort of detailed legislative revision. You know, an amendment to the Motor Vehicle Dealers' Act. The problem is they'd bring in an amendment bill, and the committees were hopelessly resourced, so no one ever did a brief on why we actually had the Motor Vehicle Dealers' Act. So how could we know anything about the bill?

I said to Jonathan, 'I'm just wasting my time, I'm bored to tears, and I don't want to do it.' I think he felt that was a bit odd because it was supposed to be a prestigious committee. I stuck with Foreign Affairs and got on with what I was interested in.

Fran Wilde

For a start I'd loosen up on the Whip.

The way Parliament works is stupid. Once I decided to get out, it became even clearer just how ludicrous the whole show is. There's a lot of pettiness. There's a lot of nonsensical behaviour in the House which is just not adult. If people behaved like that at school it would not be acceptable.

You have grown men and women—who are actually quite responsible people themselves—behaving in this bizarre way because of the restrictions put on them by the system. When you get right down to the nitty-gritty, people come here because they want to change things. They are normally people with fairly strong drives and personalities and egos. They get here and, unless they're in Cabinet, they can't do a thing.

They have absolutely no power to make any changes and they have to do what the inner clique tells them to do. Any Government is really just the senior members. So in the end the frustration of other MPs gets translated into quite juvenile behaviour.

People might say I'm shooting myself in the foot by leaving now, because if we win next time I would be one of the senior members of the Government. But I have a feeling I would want to run the place differently from how some of my colleagues would want to run it, and I don't think I'd be in the majority.

For a start I'd loosen up on the Whip. I'd give more power to the back-benches, whether they be Government or Opposition. More power back to Parliament, in fact.

When I was a Whip I argued for that with Geoffrey Palmer. We did make a lot of changes to the system in terms of select committees and other things. One of the suggestions I made was to change the system so that major issues went to Caucus before they went to Cabinet. If a suggestion was just totally unacceptable then the minister would have to go away and change it to try and accommodate the views of others. I feel that if you can't convince your colleagues of the wisdom of a suggestion, you're hardly likely to be able to get public support. In saying this I'm not suggesting a populist approach. Governments must govern. But they should also remember that they are elected.

My suggestion was not considered a wise thing to do. Cabinet unity and the ability of Cabinet to drive through even the most unpopular decisions even on trivial issues was considered to be of prime importance to the survival of the Government. In the end it was an inability to win the hearts and minds of the people that brought about the downfall of the [Labour] Government.

Michael Cullen and I were the Whips, and I believe we worked quite hard and quite well. I did a lot of work as a liaison between Cabinet and Caucus. Of course in retrospect it didn't make enough difference. The steam built up, and I think a lot of that could have been avoided if we'd had a Cabinet that had a different style of operating.

Roger Douglas didn't care, in the sense that I feel he wasn't a typical politician. He was an ideologue. He knew what he wanted to do, what he thought best for New Zealand, and he was going to do it—right or wrong. Muldoon was different. The reason he survived so long is he always curried popular support. He also ran the economy into the ground.

Her Worship, Fran Wilde, speaking after her inauguration as the first woman Mayor of Wellington, October 1992.

I asked for the job of Whip because I missed out on Cabinet. They kept Helen Clark out that year too. Helen behaved herself for the next three years and got rehabilitated but I didn't. Even though I was Whip and I worked very hard, I still continued to tell them what I thought—both privately and in Caucus. They didn't like that.

One of the multiple reasons I've chosen to move out of this place—even though I'll still be a politician—is that it gets harder and harder to be a real person in Parliament. I see the other job—the mayoralty—as being more in touch. A journalist said to a friend of mine, 'Oh, everyone's voting for Fran because she's flawed like the rest of us.' That's true, and there's no point in pretending you're anything else.

Over the last few weeks I've been campaigning for the mayoralty and I've only been here when I've had to be—question time and so on. But mostly I've come and gone as I wanted, which is more like the way other people behave, in the sense that they're allowed to go outside at lunch-time or have a doctor's appointment or walk along Lambton Quay after five o'clock. But MPs aren't allowed because they've got to be in the House. So the sense of isolation is not always the politician's fault.

Constituents' problems vary from electorate to electorate. The number one problem I get is immigration. In particular I have a lot of Asians coming to me and I have also had a number of gay couples. They're pretty tough to get through because some immigration officials can be terribly homophobic. I've also observed a degree of racism amongst some of them. I've had terrible run-ins with the Immigration Service. It's the only department where I regularly end up yelling down the phone

Annette King

... sometimes it made you want to cry ...

I didn't realize that I was going to take on such a large social worker's role, which, if you do the job properly, is the major part of the work you do in the electorate. It's easy to be the person who goes to openings of all the bowling clubs, that sort of thing. But the real work is when you sit down with people who want you to help them do things. I didn't realize there was so much of that sort of work. Once I got into the variety of roles I found it really the most enjoyable job I've ever had. It was frustrating and sometimes it made you want to cry, but it was very, very rewarding work.

Margaret Austin

I hate the word 'power' . . . because the essence of the job is service . . .

One of the first things that I started to think about was just what does this job entail? I knew there were three facets to what you were going to do. One was the representative, and that entailed being available in the electorate, being on tap. You knew you were going to be exposing your family to telephone calls at all hours of the day and night. When you're in Christchurch, you were also going to have to cope with being involved in the electorate and the community to a much greater extent than you would be when you were working, as well as running a home.

Secondly, there was the work up here. In spite of the fact that people don't understand the culture of the place, I knew the House was not the most important part of one's work up here. It was the select committee process and the scrutiny of legislation which was important. Being in Government, that side of it was going to be really fascinating—being involved in the translation of policy into implementation.

Then the third part of the job, which I call the ceremonial part, is the fact that people expect you to represent them on public occasions and to speak for them and speak to them about the things that are on your mind when the occasion arises. That's damned hard work, keeping up with the speech writing.

I hate the word 'power'. I've never been able to cope with it because the essence of the job is service, and that's how I see it. Now if that service involves being involved in decision making, that is an enormous responsibility. I think that's quite a different context for the use of the word power than thinking of it in terms of control.

There is a public perception that people are very badly behaved in the House, because they don't seem to comprehend that the House is a debating chamber. And the debate is vigorous when there are issues in contention and issues upon which there is total disagreement. How can you engage in debate on contentious issues if there isn't a clash of both personality and issues? The debating chamber is where you have the opportunity to raise all of those things.

In the select committee you hear the evidence, organize your thoughts, you respond to the wealth of information which comes through, which leads you either to have your own position reinforced, or perhaps to change it. When we were in Government and I was the chairperson of the Education and Science Select Committee there was not a single piece of legislation that

Hon. Margaret Austin, MP for Yaldhurst, 1984–; Minister of Internal Affairs, Minister of Arts and Culture, Minister of Civil Defence, Minister of Research, Science and Technology, 1990.

came through that wasn't subjected to the closest scrutiny and amendment, as a result of the select committee process. If you were to ask me what my greatest disappointment has been, it is that people did not realize the extent to which they were consulted right through our term in Government. And the extent to which decisions which were made on legislation reflected— before they were written, and then after, as a result of the select committee process—that that public scrutiny had had a very direct bearing on what eventually emerged in legislation.

I was Senior Whip. You're responsible to the Leader for ensuring that the whereabouts of everybody is known. You really are responsible for maintaining the numbers, and that requires a lot of organization. Nobody can leave this place between ten in the morning and ten-thirty at night without the permission of the Whips in duplicate and written in the book.

One copy gets sent back to them and you retain one. And they are required to say what it is they are proposing to do, exactly what time they are going to be away, because if you do that you give an undertaking that you will not leave before and you will be back on the dot that you say.

That's very important, because you've got to make sure the select committees are serviced by Members, so if you let too many people away on a Tuesday or Wednesday morning you're running short of people for your select committee. So you've got to keep that in mind when you're granting leave, you've got to make sure you've got the numbers in the House for votes, you've also got to make sure you're aware of the sort of legislation that's coming up so you've got a range of people there who are knowledgeable about the likely issues.

I learned a great deal from being the Whip. About disciplining myself, because I really worked very long hours to keep up with the electorate, which was a busy one. I was determined not to let go of select committee work so I continued to be chairperson of the Education and Science Select Committee. And the administrative work was time-consuming. But I was accustomed to organizing people anyway, so it didn't worry me.

But it is a burdensome job and nobody should underestimate it. I had good relationships with almost everybody. And people are very good when you have to turn them down for leave, or call them back when you've granted leave because something's happened. People are really very co-operative.

Marie Hasler

We're a lot more accessible now than MPs ever were before.

Life in the electorate is never boring. People come to you for absolutely anything, for help with a government department or sometimes unusual things. You never know what's going to be thrown up.

I enjoy the community work in the electorate. Before I was an MP I didn't realize the community work that went on, it's quite staggering. There's so much you get involved with—school work, boards of trustees, mental health groups, immigration issues, over-sixties. Churches do an enormous amount of welfare work in the community.

I get called on for various things. This morning I helped a soccer club that was having a bit of trouble with their fields. So I've been along to see if I can hurry it along a bit. Something that seems like a little thing is important to someone.

The job of MPs has probably changed over the years. They used to be the last port of call, now they're often the first. We're a lot more accessible now than MPs ever were before. Here I am in a shop on a main road. Anyone could come in the door and say, 'Hello, can I see the MP?'

When people say we need fewer MPs they forget the type of job it is. When I'm not here, my electorate secretary Helen is my representative. She has a very busy time on the phones, making appointments and organizing a lot of things for me. Often these have to do with departments like Social Welfare, Housing, and Accident Compensation. She does an awful lot of work.

In your first term you're pretty focused on what you're doing and it's a great learning experience. We have had a pretty tumultuous time. The thing you're really concentrating on is being the best MP you can be and getting that right. I haven't thought about a Cabinet post. Naturally, in the future it would be nice. I'd welcome the responsibility, given that I could still look after the electorate.

It's good to have responsibility for changing something for the better. As a Cabinet minister you obviously have a lot more opportunity to change things, so that would be quite satisfying. It would be wonderful to be education minister. I know that's a terribly unpopular job, because teachers never seem to like what the government's doing, but I think education is very important. I've never been a teacher, but I do think it has enormous consequences for oncoming generations.

I would love to get involved in foreign affairs; I'm very interested in our relationships with other countries. But when you're an MP you're interested in everything. Gradually as your period goes on you tend to narrow your focus. It's impossible to be an expert in everything; you soon prioritize the things you're most interested in. I've also been on the committee involved with the electoral law changes, and that's been wonderful.

It'll be exciting this year to make MMP work, if that's the option chosen. We can be a lot more focused on how it will work, the ramifications of how the party lists are made up, and how many MPs there'll be.

Parliament is pretty much the way I thought it would be, although the running of the House was a bit different to what I expected. Everything's sort of orchestrated in Parliament. You don't have much spontaneous debate; that was the thing I thought there would be more of.

A lot of legislation is pretty well decided by the time it's heard in the House. I was told before I went in that select committees are the most satisfying part of the job. I didn't realize how true that was. You sometimes get a bipartisan approach working with Labour. You make decisions and you really feel you're achieving something.

The nature of the select committees shouldn't change with MMP. There may be more parties represented on them depending how many are in the Government. I'd like to see select committees completely independent of Caucus. At the moment they're not as independent as I'd like. A lot of good work goes on in them, and it's an opportunity to get input from the public. After all that's their function.

Lianne Dalziel

You do your forty-hour week in the three days that you're here, and everything you do back in your electorate you do on top of that.

I don't know how you improve it. Maybe debates should be shorter, maybe there should be an encouragement for people to say what they need to say without having to meet time limits. On the first reading, the first speaker speaks for ten minutes and subsequent speakers for five minutes; in a report back from committee you speak for five. On the second reading, the first speaker speaks for twenty minutes, subsequent speakers for fifteen minutes, then five again. On the third reading you speak for ten minutes. They're set times that you're given to speak. You find yourself repeating a lot as a result.

It would be better if Parliament wound up on Thursday night. If we were finished by eight o'clock at night then I could fly home. That would be a saving to the taxpayer because it would mean we'd get one less overnight allowance.

You do your forty-hour week in the three days that you're here, and everything you do back in your electorate you do on top of that. It does get wearing. I normally don't leave here before eleven. The House rises at ten-thirty; normally I've got things to catch up on. But I've stayed here till one or two in the morning sometimes. It just depends.

When we're in urgency it's horrible: nine in the morning until midnight. I can't believe that they used to sit in Parliament around the clock. It's a psychological thing, I think. It's utterly unnecessary. You're just not at your best when you're debating those sort of hours.

Christine Fletcher

I can't just stand up and defend something if I don't believe in it.

I think probably because I'd had my business background to draw from, I wasn't so shocked by sexism in Parliament. It was an extension of what I'd learnt. I went in with very clear goals. Marilyn Waring had said to me whatever you do, when you go in there just stick to two issues, don't try to take on the world, otherwise you'll burn out.

For me, one issue was electoral reform. Because whatever you do, whatever you explore by way of frustrations within the system at the moment, you come back to confrontational politics. It's at the core of the problem. Electoral reform is the number one issue in terms of working towards a more co-operative environment where women can be heard and their wishes taken into consideration. I suppose I plotted to make sure I got put on the Electoral Law Committee.

When the committee structure was put out, there were no women on it. I went rushing up to the Whips' office and said, 'Look, you're giving consideration to a referendum and you do not have a woman's voice on this committee—you must.' So they responded by putting Marie Hasler and myself on to that committee.

Another strong motivation that I had was to achieve recognition for the importance of the productive sector so that industry would have a voice. I think the role that the productive sector plays in terms of providing employment has been ignored for some years. I don't know that I've been entirely successful on that count.

These were the things that really motivated me. If it meant that your ideas might be six months ahead of someone else's and you have to sow a seed and somebody else will pick it up, then so be it. What am I here for? Is it to change things or for personal glory? Sure, it's nice to get the recognition for things that you've done. But if your intention is really working within the structure to achieve change, then it doesn't really matter who finally does it.

I see the way that the House operates as a bit of a farce, in that the decisions are already made before they get into the House. I mean the House is really . . . It's a lot of hot air that goes on. If you're in Opposition maybe it's different . But so far I only have the experience of being in Government. It's at the policy stage with the minister and the Caucus committee, and fleshing out what the policy might be, where you can be most influential.

What I continue to find quite soul-destroying is that, because the House itself is a farce and, because it is so confrontational with all the political point-scoring that goes on, I know I don't perform as well. The type of person who shines in that environment can be a kind of political bully, you know? It's the Richard Prebbles who are really going to star in that kind of environment.

I could give you a couple of National Party examples too. I'm trying to think of who the worst offender might be. Sir Robert Muldoon helped create that environment and Richard Prebble has moulded himself within it. He actually aspired to be like him. They are the kind of people who really shine in that environment.

A weakness I could be accused of is that I find it really hard to speak convincingly with passion and vigour in the House if I don't really believe in something. I can't just stand up and defend something if I don't believe in it. I'm not good at playing those games. So in many ways I know that I am probably more effective at the policy implementation level.

It all comes back to the need to have electoral reform. It would be wonderful if we were all Members of the House of Representatives, we all represented our electorates, we didn't have all the party voting on things and we had some conscience votes.

But it doesn't work like that. When I tried to get on the Standing Orders Committee—the committee which determines the way in which the House of Parliament can operate—I was told that until you've had a couple of terms in this place you don't have a contribution to make to this committee. When I criticized the way that the House sitting hours work, one Member even went so far as to say, 'Look, if you can't take the heat then get out of the frying pan.' But how can you balance your life effectively when the whole issue of time management has never really been dealt with by Parliament?

Whetu Tirikatene-Sullivan

. . . this chronic under-resourcing of the vast Southern Māori electorate is an excellent example of institutional racism.

There were two Māori in the Third Labour Government: Hon. Matiu Rata and me. We were elected on the first ballot, in fact. I can only speak for myself but, as always I have never lobbied for myself—so I was suprised.

I should point out that it is a Rātana approach to refrain from lobbying for oneself, or to seek publicity for oneself. This could be said to be thoroughly inappropriate for a person in politics.

However, if one's constituents have confidence in their parliamentary representative, I would equally well conclude that a high 'popular vote' would be more significant.

So I do take some satisfaction from the fact that, in the nine parliamentary elections in which I have been a candidate (for Southern Māori), I have usually gained the highest percentage of valid votes cast of any candidate in the election. It is also satisying to have held the highest 'popular vote' of

Hon. Whetu Tirikatene-Sullivan, MP for Southern Māori, 1967–; Minister of Tourism, 1972–75; Minister for the Environment, 1974–75.

any candidate in a contested election (eighty-eight per cent).

It was not at all difficult being the only woman in Cabinet. I was greatly respected by the Prime Minister, who admired the fact that I came to my own decision as minister, allowing no permanent head to wheel decisons up to me.

I have always preferred to table a thoroughly well-researched paper in support of my case. I still do, given the time, and in an enormously under-resourced office, running what is more akin to an industry which covers two-thirds of the country.

In fact, this chronic under-resourcing of the vast Southern Māori electorate is an excellent example of institutional racism. Who would publicly declaim that it is reasonable not to provide at least one more staff member, simply to do filing?

There is no time for the media; nor time to document from my vast archives areas of significant public decison making of which I have been part.

I have, however, provided archival data to a handful of post graduate scholars; and, over the years, have provided background data to numerous questions from students doing other papers.

However, the last person asked about forty major questions in order to submit her thesis. I gave comprehensive data, which even had to be delivered to her home. I have never again heard from her, and have decided against investing time in this way again—since I might as well be writing a book.

Elizabeth Tennet

The husbands of politicians never do the work that the wives of politicians do.

The pace of reform has to slow down. I think that Parliament still needs some changes whereby we have shorter sitting hours. It seems to have become worse over the last few years, this horrendous workload. Prior to that, MPs had a pretty cushy number. I'm not suggesting that we go back to that, but the workload is just crazy now.

The support staff who were introduced by the last Labour Government have been a great help in the electorate itself. We now have electorate secretaries. But in a sense you get pulled into all sorts of issues that you mightn't even have any control over. MPs have to pace themselves. It's important and quite hard to do, because it means you have to say no to some people.

Some of the things that we're looking at for the next Labour Government, where we have a smaller Cabinet, are slowing down the pace of reform and better forward planning, which I've always been a great believer in. Possibly a few more resources in the electorate itself. But the reality is if you are an MP your whole life is being an MP, you don't do much else.

My husband John has always known I've been interested in politics, even before I declared myself as wanting to stand for Parliament. But I was pretty busy before I went into Parliament too. I worked very long hours there and I was away quite a lot. So he knew I was a fairly independent sort of person.

There's a difference between men and women going into politics. With the wives of politicians there's much more of a cultural understanding that they'll be supporting their men. Often the wives are doing a lot of the electorate work, while the men are doing their work in Wellington. Their wives provide a very supportive role, deal with constituents, and follow up their problems. Whereas with a female politician, her husband usually has his own job and there is no perception of him acting in that same role in the electorate.

Perhaps in some ways it puts a bit more work on a woman MP and her work is slightly less supported in that sense. But apart from the workload you do need the support of your spouse and an acceptance that you'll be away from your house most of the time. The husbands of politicians never do the work that the wives of politicians do. I think you'll find that with all of the women MPs.

Joy McLauchlan

If there were more women in the House I think we'd
structure Parliament differently.

Going back to cave-living and stuff, women were worrying about what they were cooking on the fire and tending one child to the breast and making sure another one didn't toddle out and get eaten by a marauding lion or whatever. So their minds were focused on several different things at once, whereas man the hunter was just singularly devoted to the issue of the moment. If you extrapolate that forward into today's world when man is now in politics, he still has that as his primary focus. Whereas women still like to have a broad range of issues and interests, and politics does not allow the time for that.

If there were more women in the House I think we'd structure Parliament differently. I think we wouldn't sit for such long hours, that we would break earlier in the evening in order to be able to get home at a more reasonable hour. I know that Ruth Richardson looked at it very seriously when she first went into Parliament. Sitting through the dinner hour and raising Parliament at eight o'clock. Perhaps we could make the hours more amenable. I also don't know about the expectations people have of their MPs. People like to see their MPs at meetings, but you're also well aware of the work that's still to be done at home or at the office desk. That's again one of the great joys of being in Opposition because you have that time to be out in public. I wonder if maybe we make work for ourselves sometimes.

Annette King

The trick is . . . to keep people around you.

If someone was interested in getting involved in politics—first of all don't be put off by the current mood towards politicians. There's a very negative view out there. A lot of people have said to me, 'Why would you want to do that? Everybody hates politicians.' If that was the case we would have to be run by computers, because no one would do the job.

But you do need to know a lot about it. It would be good to talk to someone who had done the job or who was doing the job. The really important thing is to have a lot of people who are going to help you. That includes your family and your close friends.

My campaign here in Miramar is quite different to what I had in Horowhenua where I had good support from people who'd been in politics, but it was more moral support than active support because they were all busy running their own campaigns. Here I have people helping me who have come from all over the place. Old friends. My brother-in-law is my campaign manager. He wanted to be, he wanted to help. So I've got a real group of people around me. That's really important. It makes it much more enjoyable and it takes a huge load off you. The trick is, of course, to keep people around you so that as the years go by you keep an organization that's working with you.

Margaret Moir

. . . as a woman in a very male-oriented House, I found it similar to local government and to the Coast.

It wasn't a bit like I imagined. It's certainly a very male bastion, very much so, although there are concessions. But as a woman in a very male-oriented House, I found it similar to local government and to the Coast. But I have to say the hours and the workload just blew me away, for a start.

One politician told me he measured how much correspondence came though his office in a week and multiplied that by fifty-two. It came to four storeys high! Forty-eight feet. If anybody had told me this beforehand, I'd have thought, 'Aw, go on.'

But the workload and the hours were hard, as well as just getting used to travelling.

Another thing I found quite hard was realizing I actually had to establish credibility with my fellow MPs. Even though I'd been elected I still had to gain some sort of rapport with them, especially with the ministers. And the things that I am involved in are still very male-dominated; when they say things like, 'Well, gentlemen' you have to say, 'Ah, ah' and get a wee correction. Silly things like that. It takes a while for things like that to change.

Judy Keall

*If I actually asked what it meant I often found that a
whole lot of other people didn't know either.*

I found it was a very good idea, if I wasn't sure about something, to ask
questions, particularly at select committees. You'd find everybody would be
nodding and the officials would be spouting all their expertise. Various MPs
would be using the jargon words. If I actually asked what it meant I often
found that a whole lot of other people didn't know either. It could be quite
surprising how ignorant everybody else was.

Eventually I learnt the ropes and became much more competent. I ended
up chairing select committees. In fact, after I was made Junior Whip they
asked me to stay on as chair of the Social Services Select Committee to see
through the Health Research Council and Smoke-Free Environment
legislation. It was very important they went through before the election and
I'm proud of that.

Another piece of advice I would suggest is get to know your local government department officials—what their responsibilities are—because you
might need to know how everything works and it's a bit late to be learning it
when you've got a constituency problem.

Judy Keall, MP for Glenfield, 1984–90.

It's important to keep in touch with all your community people. I used to have quite extensive mailing lists, but I also had four days in the electorate: Friday, Saturday, Sunday, Monday. I consciously scheduled appointments or visits so that I could meet up with community people. When I had visiting MPs I made sure I had meetings with volunteers in the community on particular issues, whether it was health or social work or whatever.

In the '84 campaign, particularly, I used to do a lot of shopping. I found it was a very helpful way of keeping in touch with people. But when my male opponent tried doing the same thing, the supermarket management asked him to leave because they saw it as politicking. Maybe he didn't know how to shop properly, but when he went to the supermarket he got kicked out. So women do have some advantages. It was funny because there were some weeks I shopped every day. I could spend about an hour and a half getting fifteen dollars' worth.

Katherine O'Regan

'If they were my children I'd spank their bottoms.'

Perhaps what would sum up the frustration that one has in the process is that it is slow and cumbersome, but it does work, and it's the best that we know of at the moment. I think we should perhaps adapt it a little more.

This was quite a public thing at the time although it might not have been so up in the north.When I was in Opposition I was asking a question of the Minister of Education. Mr Wellington was still in the House at the time and he started taking points of order. There must have been an altercation going on. Anyway I'd just get up to ask my supplementary question and a point of order would be made.The House was full, and it was noisy and fractious. Not unlike a kindergarten, although I think kindergartens are usually better behaved. Children are allowed to be noisy and make silly comments but as an adult you shouldn't. But it can be very amusing I have to say. However, I felt my frustration, and I eventually got the chance to stand up and ask my question and I said to Mr Speaker, 'If they were my children I'd spank their bottoms.'

It brought the House down. And Trevor de Cleene said, 'If the Member for Waipa is offering then I'll be the first.' That really was frustration. But it was most amusing, and I think they're the things that stick in your mind.

In my maiden speech I concluded, I think, with, 'Let us cease the petty jibe.' That was wonderful, wasn't it? I thought it was very grand. I managed to keep my mouth shut for six months.

I've not stopped listening to Parliament since 1973–74. I've listened continually and I think it's really no worse now than it was before. People often have the wrong idea of what Parliament actually is. It would be quite nice sometimes for the House just to settle down, but it's skittish. I reared calves as a farmer's wife, and some days the calves were quite skittish. They'd flick around the paddock and you couldn't do a thing with them. If you tried to get one or two into a certain area they'd all balk and go off somewhere else. Sometimes the House is a bit like that.

I enjoy being there. I can't resist at times being part of the 'petty jibes'. Some days I'm better at it than others. What gets to you is really the long hours after five o'clock, when everyone else is going home and relaxing. You're still at work and a lot of people don't realize that.

You have to be a night owl to be an MP. I feel sorry for people who are larks. Trying to stay awake at the other end of the day is quite tough for someone who by nature would prefer to get up at five. I've seen some Members looking pretty tired and haggard by the end of the week.

7

ISSUES

Whether as the result of a strong women's group asserting itself or as a counter to a disappearing women's vote, there was, towards the end of Labour's term, a major legislative change reflecting a specific women's agenda. Not all of it remains in place, but the new policies have had a significant impact upon our social configuration.

In the nineties major changes, promoted partly by National women MPs, have also helped create a new social and economic environment.

Marilyn Waring

It was a bear pit; it was truly disgusting.

In hindsight, I'm not sure that the experience of being one of only two women, or the only woman [in Caucus] is very different from that which women find themselves in other patriarchal institutions. Like being the only woman in major banking or the only woman on a major board.

But I didn't expect it. It was a bear pit; it was truly disgusting. I had never been in a situation where human beings behaved like that. The easiest way to describe it is to tell you a little story. There are thousands of stories like this.

I specifically remember in 1976 or '77 that there were a lot of young women breaking out of places like Miramar Girls' Home and Weymouth just weeks before they were going to be 'rehabilitated with their families'.

Since I was not much older than them and I was on the Social Welfare Committee and I was concerned, I started making a lot of visits to these homes. And it became patently obvious that the kids were not interested in being sent home to be further subjected to incidents of rape and incest. And that was why they were running away.

When I went back to the Government Caucus and said this, there was dead silence. Everybody looked at me like I'd come from another planet. One of my colleagues, who for now can remain nameless, said, 'Normal women don't think like that.' And we went on to the next agenda item.

Stories like that can only begin to tell you what it was like and it was constant. I can give you other examples for those nine years. In those days—

especially Bert Walker's period—we were hot on the domestic purposes benefit. These terrible women who ran out and got pregnant and ripped the country off.

But the abuse of the domestic purposes benefit never got near the shortfall in maintenance which the Government wasn't recovering from fathers. The first years I started bothering about it, the figure was something like twenty-three million dollars. Then it went to fifty-six million. Then it went to eighty-seven million, and it would continue to climb.

Every year in the pre-Budget debate I would come in and say this is truly ridiculous. If any other sphere of the population were indebted to the government to this extent we would imprison them. We'd have liens on their wages. We'd stop them at airports. Why don't we do this? Then I'd look around the caucus and realize some of my colleagues were in that category. So I think there has been significant progress made.

Jenny Shipley

I said I was interested in how many of the men who were there in Caucus had been present at a birth.

Women can say some things that men can't. I remember a Caucus discussion about sexually transmitted disease. I think I used some rather colourful language about the realities of chlamydia and other sexually transmitted diseases. The men believed that if you didn't tell them they wouldn't be screwing behind the bike sheds.

I said just forget it. The best you can hope to do is to give reasons why they shouldn't be sexually active. I don't think we've ever had better reasons why we should have a group of chaste young people, in terms of at least making the choice of being sexually active. I want young people to have good information so that young women know that they're running the risk of cervical cancer and the wart virus by early sexual activity. We now know a whole lot of things we didn't know in my generation. I think young women are entitled to know about that. I also think young men are entitled to know that they may be carriers of the wart virus that causes cervical cancer.

The argument was, if you didn't tell them, would they do it? And, thank goodness, at the end of the day, the majority of the Caucus—and we were in Opposition then—came around to the view that, given the reality that young people were sexually active, they needed to have the data. Or at least it shouldn't be a criminal offence to talk to them about it, so that they could then make the choices.

Another instance that was relatively funny—again it was in Opposition—where we had to decide on our position on the Midwives Bill. And on this particular day Katherine and Ruth and I were in the Caucus. Don McKinnon was the health spokesman and he started off saying this is a piece of legislation on which we have to decide a policy position.

And there were the most extraordinary speeches from a series of male colleagues. Sir Robert Muldoon, who had just come out of hospital with heart surgery, said that modern drugs were very technical and he didn't think that anyone other than GPs should be able to administer anything. He was quite sure that women didn't know what was good for them.

These speeches went on and on and on, and there was a point where the three of us just burst out laughing. We thought it was quite the funniest thing we'd ever heard. Katherine spoke first, and then I spoke, and I said I was interested in how many of the men who were there in Caucus had been present at a birth. I didn't actually ask them to put their hands up, because I thought that was going a little far.

I said it might be a surprise to you to know that GPs don't actually stand stroking women's brows for the whole of the labour. Usually they rush in the door about time to catch the baby as the damn thing's due to be delivered and in reality don't have a blind bit to do with the actual process of birthing.

The fact that they then get paid a very significant amount of money is one of the gross anomalies historically and it's time it was changed. Quite apart from women's preference in having a midwife who supports you prior to, and in the middle, and after.

It was hugely funny because it actually dawned on them afterwards when they realized. There were some who were quite rigid. Others saw that you get so used to listening to your own rhetoric it becomes absolute garbage. There were a number who thought their experiences in hospital should override women's desire to be treated as they wish to be treated .

Whetu Tirikatene-Sullivan

The horrifying fact is that violence and sexual exploitation are viewed as acceptable entertainment.

Whatever the system, we should reserve seats for Māori. It's really as simple as that. The number should be determined according to a formula which recognizes the Māori population. A while ago, I drafted a private member's bill increasing the number of Māori electorates from four to seven. Were I introducing the bill now, I would make it ten seats.

Not only are Māori the indigenous people, they are the tāngata whenua. It must never be forgotten that, under the Treaty of Waitangi—which marked the beginning of constitutional government in the nation—the Crown formally recognized the existing rights of the Māori tāngata whenua, and undertook to protect them.

The origin of Māori representation in 1867 was not in recognition of the fact that the Treaty was the genesis of this nation. That should have been the reason. However, it fortuitously and belatedly provided for Māori advocacy in the New Zealand House of Representatives. Otherwise, there might have been no designated Māori advocacy. If the Electoral Reform Bill, as introduced to Parliament, goes through without any reservation for Māori constituencies, we might again have none. On the other hand, we might have more. But that is left entirely to chance.

Recent local government elections and the elections for school boards of trustees did not see many Māori candidates returned. As a Treaty partner, we ought not leave our fortunes to be determined in the same way—by the decision of the majority. We are not just any minority in New Zealand. We are the tāngata whenua. We are the Treaty partner.

Another of my preoccupations has been the protection of children against all forms of violence. This has merged with my sense of anger at violence against women. All forms of exploitation of these two groups fill me with outrage.

I was one of a handful which met in Christchurch to set up New Zealand's first support group for battered wives. Other members were Sister O'Regan and Dr Doris Church. Directly as a result, a private member's bill was drafted and eventually introduced by my colleague, Mrs Mary Batchelor. All of this preceded any other such group in New Zealand, although many eventually followed and have become part of the New Zealand social landscape. This is an indictment of the violence of men in our community.

My most recent private member's bill is aimed at reducing the level of violence depicted on television. The horrifying fact is that violence and sexual exploitation are viewed as acceptable entertainment. All I can say is that, among the men I know, those with the most guts are also non-violent; my husband Denis being one of them. Violence flashes when there is no self-control; or where the personality is immature, fractured, and inadequately developed. It is encouraged in an atmosphere which is chauvinistic, which claims possession of the female sex. Group rape is the most cowardly expression of this. New Zealand society has a long way to go to be rid of this macho cancer.

I am especially outraged when children are the target—but there will always be those adults who, given the right to determine what shall be censored, will consider it to be the human right of mature males to enjoy pornographic videos and the like. This glamorizes the ultimate violence against women—yes, and even against children. Thus have males become desensitized. Serial rapists and murderers have specified pornographic videos as the trigger for their rampaging. There are many battles yet to be fought and won in that area.

Helen Clark

There were a million things going on.

When David Lange made his portfolio allocations after '87 he moved Michael Bassett from health, I suspect because Michael Bassett was so close to Roger Douglas. Bassett had agreed to have Alan Gibbs run a task force on hospitals, and it looked very much as though the New Right agenda was on the boil there. So Lange hacked Bassett from that portfolio and put Caygill in. Caygill is a person who is dry and pro-market on the economy but not on social policy. That wouldn't have been apparent to a lot of people, but Lange recognized it. Caygill, by his own admission, took a long time to come to grips with the portfolio and understand it.

Rt. Hon. Helen Clark, MP for Mt Albert, 1981–; Minister of Conservation, Minister of Housing, 1987–89; Minister of Health, Minister of Labour 1989–90; Deputy Prime Minister, 1989–90. Photograph taken during a visit to a primary school in the Mt Albert electorate, 1990.

But he had a background in local government on the Christchurch City Council and he believed in local people being able to make decisions on the shape of their health services, and he didn't believe in corporatizing. So when the Gibbs report came along, Caygill said, 'Well, it's all very interesting.' Then he coughed and put it on the shelf and life went on.

So at least when I came on it was different from coming into housing and finding that the thing was just about to be lost and then to spend eighteen months fending that off. With health, no damage had been done to the public policy framework of the health system. That was of great assistance.

But it was very destabilizing changing ministers halfway through the term of office, because everything takes a while to learn and there were just a lot of things that had to be done. It was a hectic period, setting up area health boards, working out charters and goals and trying to do something about a Health Commission and Smoke-free and the Health Research Council. There were a million things going on.

A lot of them relate to a long-term womens' health agenda. Like promotion of wellness and the Smoke-free Environment Act. And changing from a Medical Research Council to a Health Research Council, taking away the excessive biomedical focus on finding cures to illnesses and trying to turn that around. I'd say that was a pretty basic theme in the twenty-month period. It was quite a revolutionary approach to the health portfolio.

I made a lot of enemies. The pharmaceutical industry actively campaigned against Labour in the last election. Full-page ads in New Zealand metropolition papers, implying that Labour's policies amounted to euthanasia. Then there was the whole tobacco thing. The alcohol industry funded National rather than Labour.

The Medical Association of course went crazy with High Court reviews and the rest of it. The Medical Association worked quite co-operatively with me as minister, but that was before I'd disclosed my hand on what might be done for primary medical subsidies, which was a pretty complicated area, and needed a lot of policy work.

In the '87 Budget we worked up to the idea of having voluntary contracts so that we could actually guarantee that people could have affordable doctors if they wanted them. We calculated that over time that there would be enough doctors who wanted to take the contract to ensure that. But the Medical Association has always fought against any notion of capping fees, so that, even if doctors wanted to voluntarily cap fees, as clearly some did because they signed the contracts, this was considered to be such a fundamental breach of doctors' freedom that they went hysterical.

After the '87 Budget they filed in the High Court for having the contracts struck down on the grounds that it was *ultra vires*. That I'd exceeded my powers in law as the Minister of Health; that I didn't have the power to do what I had done. They lost. Justice Thomas in the High Court struck down their case on every single point. But that just made them more vindictive.

Then we had the business where Dr Ridley-Smith did a scurrilous leaflet which they delivered to everyone in my electorate in the week leading up to the election. If he had got away with that, then anyone was vulnerable to smear attacks. I survived it because I had a large majority which, while severely pared, still had enough to carry me through. A lot of people couldn't have survived that sort of attack.

Dr Ridley-Smith was found guilty of criminal libel. He took advice from the Medical Association who assured him that the statements in the leaflets were true. Tom Marshall came to his defence on the front page of the *New Zealand Herald*, two days before the election when the leaflet was out, saying that the statements were true. Marshall was deputy head of the Medical Association and gave evidence at the trial.

Ridley-Smith was just not a credible witness. And the judge was virtually speechless. The penalty in law was pitiful. It was three months in jail or a thousand-dollar fine. He got a fine, I think it was about seven hundred and fifty dollars. He never appealed, but their behaviour was outrageous.

He just went too far, I probably should have sued him in civil court as well. I had offers to take the case, on a sort of shares basis with the takings, but I decided not to. My objective was for him to be found guilty in the eyes of the law. To be seen to be pursuing money would have been perceived to be vindictive and possibly greedy. But I achieved my objective.

Smoke-free was another battle. Initially in the Cabinet there was no great difficulty. There was general agreement that smoking was a bad thing, and David Caygill had been very interested in it as Minister of Health. He was finance minister and carried a lot of weight. But, as the public controversy over it mounted, I could feel that general support wasn't quite what it had been. In the end we carried on. I actually made up my mind that if there was an attempt to have it dropped I would have resigned. Because I'm not prepared to go out on a limb for something with support and then see the limb cut off behind me.

It was perceived by some as an electoral liability, but we were able to show that we won as many votes as we lost on it. The public opposition was entirely orchestrated by groups funded and organized by the tobacco industry. Sadly, they brought in behind them people in the arts and sporting community who should have known better, people who couldn't see past the the dollars they got from the tobacco industry. In the fullness of time the opposition crumbled, and, when the National Government decided not repeal the sponsorship provision, there was hardly a whimper at all.

But in 1990 a tremendous amount of money was poured into it by tobacco companies. They had the same international public relations firm working for them as they had had in Canada two or three years before when similar legislation was up. So clearly the tobacco industry put a good deal of emphasis on trying to beat it back in New Zealand because, if it happened here, then other countries might stand up to them. Of course now Australia has gone the same way. There's more happening in Europe.

They had every reason to try and stop it on the beaches here but they didn't. I do think if the issue had not been in the hands of a very senior Cabinet minister it never would have proceeded. I had to stake all my clout and reputation on it, and even then I had to deal with wobbly knees. It had come to the point where I was thinking, 'any more of this and I'm going'.

Appointing Ken Gray to the Sponsorship Council was a tremendous help. Another MP came up with the name when he knew I was looking for someone, but I thought it was inspired. Of course, Ken had been an All Black and he had fairly broad community involvement. He really got into it, and he was very good with the people who were sponsored. He made an effort to go out to their functions and gave pep talks after the game, that sort of thing. We did appoint a very good Council and that made the whole idea much more acceptable over the next two or three years.

Pay equity came out of the Labour Women's Council and the work of Margaret Wilson. I think it was in the '87 manifesto to do something about employment equity. After the '87 election, Geoffrey reorganized Cabinet committes and set up what was called the Social Equity Committee and then set up about twenty-two different reviews and working parties. One of them was on this.

Eventually the proposals came up. Of course they were strongly resisted by the Treasury, the State Services Commission, the Ministry of Commerce, and the Labour Department. Apart from the Ministry of Women's Affairs, there was no institutional support for it so nothing happened.

When I became Minister of Labour it was with the expectation that I would do something. It was a campaign pledge, so I had to do something about it and hence the bill. Even at the point, when the bill was drawn up, Cabinet and the Labour Department and the State Services Commission were still writing submissions against it. Which, when you consider I was Minister of Labour, was pretty extraordinary.

The Labour Department would have liked to deregulate the labour market some more anyway. Certainly the last thing they wanted was to insert some new regulation by way of independent bodies and arbitration on wage rights, which was what it amounted to. It was resisted down to the wire.

But we'd also changed finance ministers. David Caygill was personally supportive of it. It wasn't too much of a struggle by then because I wanted it and I was the Deputy Prime Minister. The Minister of Finance supported it. A lot of things fell into line at that point. I think Roger Douglas was back in the Cabinet, but he wasn't in a crucial position.

I never quite believed Birch when he said he'd repeal pay equity before Christmas, but he did. And he did it by introducing a bill two weeks before Parliament rose. It went to a select committee which sort of sat from ten in the morning until midnight. They heard submissions, virtually all against it.

I think the select committee were pretty shocked. Because all these groups were coming in and saying, 'This is absolutely outrageous', particularly on the equal employment opportunities side of it. They agreed to go back to their Caucus and recommend that the bill not proceed.

They went back to the Caucus and Birch basically told them to grow up. So they came back, deliberated on the bill. And the bill was reported back as it was and it went through under urgency. The election was on the twenty-seventh of October and the bill was through and passed before Christmas. So it was one of the first things they did.

Margaret Shields

[Politics is] not about having power yourself, it's about empowering other people.

I was on a ministerial trip, up in Waverley, and there was a group of Māori women who had gathered to meet with us. They had some sort of work group, and they were very respectful, very welcoming, and my private secretary introduced me, and then I spoke a little about how important it was to get input into women's policy. Then after a few questions a rather shy, but articulate Māori woman got up, an older woman, and she said they didn't really understand about policy.

And I talked about it and I got round to the old feminist slogan, 'politics is personal and the personal is political'. I said, 'That sounds like jargon, but what it really means is that you can ignore policy but policy won't ignore you.'

And I said all the things that you've talked about like the work you're doing for women, the impact of cost of living on your family life, the young people—all those things are either the consequence of policy or can be affected by policy. I told them, 'If you share the effects of these policies with us we can do something about it.'

And the woman just lit up like a candle and so did all her mates. We had a great discussion and it was really hard getting away. Because they suddenly realized that they could do something. And to me that's exactly what being in politics is about. It's not about having power yourself, it's about empowering other people.

The thing that always gave me the biggest charge was when I ran across people who were doing great things. And I'd say, 'How did you get started?' And they'd turn around and say, 'Don't you remember?' And then they'd tell me we'd had a talk about this ten or fifteen years ago. And they'd thought, 'Well, she's a pretty ordinary person, if she can do it then so can I.'

Now that's really important: instead of just getting on our high horse actually supporting other people. There are outstanding politicians who stand head and shoulders above the rest of us, but most of us are pretty ordinary.

And nothing ever happens because one person decides—even if people try to make it like that. The best policies are the result of an awful lot of people wanting change.

The nuclear policy is an example of that. The Labour Party would not have changed the policy unless they'd had the vast majority of New Zealanders behind them. And that happened because people had been working for many years in New Zealand in small groups, coming together into larger groups, going out and proselytizing. And it's that kind of grass-roots process that to me is real politics.

One of the things that was really satisfying for me was getting the early childhood education policy into place. Getting to the point where we have a way of supporting the further development of kōhanga reo. One of the things that I brought with me to the Dominican Republic is a set of photographs of the signing of the agreement with the Kōhanga Reo Trust.

One thing I feel even more strongly about is that New Zealand doesn't know what it's good at. One of the things it's good at is participatory development; developments that come up from the grass roots rather from the top down. Kōhanga reo is a wonderful example of that.

Nuclear-free was something of which we felt enormously proud. Pay equity was one that was a sting in the tail because it was the first thing that the present Government decided to repeal.

Joy McLauchlan

If people are being debased or dehumanized or
degraded, as a Government we do have a role.

There is co-operation on some issues like pornography. But even with that there's quite a wide diversity among women as to how far we should go on the censorship issue. Some people have quite firmly held views on censorship.

I suppose being in politics has really taught me that it is all about balance. I used to hold very strong views on the fact that we shouldn't be able to have IRD or Social Welfare linkages. That privacy had to be paramount. But then I looked at taxpayers' dollars being abused and defrauded, and I realized we've got to have some form of highly controlled but available means of determining who is abusing the system.

And in terms of conservation, what right do we have to be able to tell people what they can do on their private land? But, in terms of the long-term future or of people who might live upwind or downstream of those people, we do have a requirement to say, 'No, you can't do whatever you like on your own land.' Or in your own home when it comes to how you treat your family. Some people feel very strongly, and I used to too, that what you do in your own home is your privilege and your right. But that's not true. If people are being debased or dehumanized or degraded, as a Government we do have a role.

You walk a fairly narrow tightrope sometimes between what is appropriate and what is not. And the public mind changes a lot, between what they consider to be appropriate and what they do not. National has traditionally reacted to the public feeling, whereas in many ways Labour has endeavoured to lead it. We've always been accused in the National Government of being one that seeks power by any measure at all in order to retain power. I'd say the last two years put the lie to that little theory.

I think Michael Cox said it: as a politician you alight on issues like a butterfly and you deal with them and then you zip off to the next one. There's often little time to get into detailed involvement with things. I think of some of the things I went into Parliament to try and change; I have not been able to devote that time to it.

I'd like a greater awareness of complementary medicine, for instance. Of the effects on food and health of pesticides. Whenever I try and bring them up the reaction to it is, 'Aw, yeah, she's been got at by the cranks.' But I think it's a very real issue. A lot of our problems can be directly related to what we are eating and breathing, and I think we need to be able to put more emphasis on to that.

Censorship we're finally getting a hold of, so I'm quite happy about that. I'd like to have a far greater awareness; a very public programme on the results of sex being unwanted children. Every child has the right to be a wanted child, born into a wanted family. We're going to have to be more explicit about the needs of society in that area. We have to put the role of the child in a far more premier position than we have. Just because you have a child doesn't mean you have the right to continue on as you would like in your life, because the child does change that.

Elizabeth Tennet

It was very sad to see that the very first thing that the Tories did in 1990 was to repeal that pay equity legislation.

Being in Parliament is not easy for anyone. There have been people whom I have admired. Margaret Wilson and Helen Clark were always two women whom I have respected greatly for what they have been able to achieve. I respected Ann Hercus for her toughness and decision making.

I was thrilled with the implementation of the pay equity and EEO legislation, and I worked quite extensively on that issue. I felt that was a real milestone. It's something that I and others had been arguing for through the Clerical Workers' Union. It was really satisfying to see the campaign going through the union structures into the political process, through the party policy, and then finally implemented in Parliament. That was very satisfying for me personally. I was just one of many people who worked hard and

Hon. Dame Ann Hercus, MP for Lyttelton, 1978–87; Minister of Police, Minister of Social Welfare, Minister of Women's Affairs, 1984–87.

pushed the extra funding for child care through. So that was also very satisfying. Those were really high points.

It was very sad to see that the very first thing that the Tories did in 1990 was to repeal that pay equity legislation. Pay equity was seen to be a very middle-class sort of thing, which was a shame because it would have greatly helped clothing workers and women working in restaurants and those sorts of areas.

We had quite heavy discussions amongst ourselves about how the legislation would end up. I know from my own point of view I was determined that it wouldn't just skim across middle-class women and give them a few more opportunities. It would help the women in the low-paid jobs. And that legislation did that. But because it was in for such a short time it never really got past the first round of negotiations, and so that understanding never penetrated to those people. The other thing is that a lot of the unions didn't really understand it and there wasn't enough time to really sell it.

We've got to expect the employers' group coming out saying that it's unworkable and being opposed to it. At the women's meetings that I and the other women MPs were able to attend, it was very well received. But it's getting it out to the women of New Plymouth and these other areas.

Marie Hasler

Certain things are regarded as women's issues, but I think they're people's issues.

Some people are suprised if we come out on something that a woman isn't expected to comment on. Certain things are regarded as women's issues but I think they're people's issues.

For example, I thought pay equity was a meaningless piece of legislation. It was very cleverly worded to sound wonderful, but I don't think it would have gained a thing. It's crazy to think that just by calling something pay equity you're going to get everyone paid the same. It's ridiculous. It was just clever publicity. There are more fundamental things that have to be changed for women. After all, men don't have equity. Life isn't fair, life isn't equitable.

The philosophy behind pay equity was like saying, 'Nurses are paid a lot less than police because nurses are mostly women and why should they be paid less?' That was sort of the principle of it. In other words, should a nurse's work be on a par with policeman's or a fireman's work? They argued that women's pay had been downgraded.

I'm all for upgrading women's worth. I'm very pro-women. But how do you legislate for equity? How do you compare jobs with jobs? It's often market-driven. It's supply and demand. It's very hard to get round that with legislation. It gets very artificial when you start comparing apples with pears. You've got to equip yourself with something that's in demand, that's the first thing. We've got too many lawyers and too many accountants. You've got to think, what is going to get me a good job? Women need to think about all this at an early age; to be quite calculating about it.

Jenny Kirk

You get those networks going.

Politics at its best is enormously satisfying. You can do a great deal to help other people or to change society. I found it satisfying to be responsible for getting more Lottery Board funding for projects like the Awataha Marae and the Auckland Maritime Museum. It was satisfying to help with the Chelsea Sugar Works' problems with deregulation.

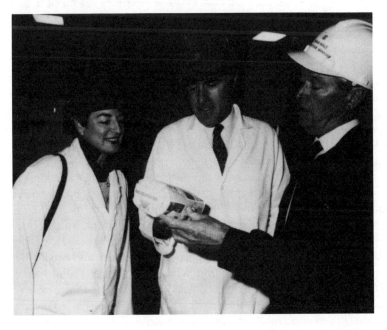

Jenny Kirk, MP for Birkenhead, 1987–90, touring Chelsea Sugar Works with former Prime Minister, Sir Geoffrey Palmer.

Another example is the assistance a back-bench MP can give a minister. I chaired the Health Caucus when Helen Clark was health minister. She took a lot of flak on the smoke-free legislation, but we backed her up and gave a heap of support.

There were a huge number of people out there giving her support all the time, publicly. And it was essential to make sure those people understood that they needed to give support. Not only do you need your personal support, but you get those networks going to make sure that they are writing letters into the papers and giving you the public support that is required to make sure a policy you agree with goes ahead.

Annette King

The positive side of the portfolio, for me, was the starting of community employment development.

Some people say it's a death-warrant, but I actually asked for the employment portfolio. For two years I'd been the under-secretary to Phil Goff, and so I'd spent most of my time actually working with unemployed people. My job was to go around and be the ears and eyes and legs. There were so many good ideas for local economic development and community employment, and I really wanted to be responsible for starting some of them. We didn't have much in that sort of line in employment policy, and I could see some exciting things.

People were showing me these really positive things they could do to generate employment, and so I was keen to have the opportunity to do it, combined with the contacts I'd made. The negative side of it was commenting on the unemployment figures every month. That was awful because every month you just knew there were going to be more people out of work. You had to try to find positiveness and there's very little positive about people being out of work. But the positive side of the portfolio, for me, was the starting of community employment development, which we did get going and some really good things happened.

Unfortunately a lot of it doesn't happen now. It started with people like Peter Kenyon, who came over here from Western Australia and helped set up the Community Employment Development Unit within the Department of Labour. It really got people motivated. He was very controversial as far as the Department was concerned. He wasn't a bureaucrat. His job had been to get employment intitiatives going for the Western Australian Government, and he'd been very successful and I'd met him and I was very keen to have him.

When he got here the Department was very suspicious of him because he didn't believe in big bureaucracies. He wanted people who were on the ground working to create employment, not sitting in government departments. Several weeks before the election his contract expired and they didn't renew him, knowing I was going to go if the Labour Government was going to lose. Everybody knew that by then.

The interesting thing is that the job that I finally got at the Enterprise Board was at the implementation edge of the policies that we'd been putting in place. So I've actually had two years making them work which has been wonderful, because it wasn't just theory. I could see how they could work. They'd worked in other places, and how they were all working in an *ad hoc* way in New Zealand. What we did was to put some government resources behind them.

There was an Advisory Committee on the Employment of Women that had been in place for some time and had some very good women on it. But very little notice was taken of them. It was lip service in my view. In that year that I was minister we actually tried to get together an employment policy for women. It wasn't as successful as I wanted it to be because it was done too much within the bureaucracy. And also it wasn't long enough. The ideas had just been put together. Margaret Wilson and several others had done a really good report on ways that we could improve employment for women. But there wasn't time to implement it, and I haven't seen anything that's happened from it since.

Katherine O'Regan

What more could you want than to be Minister of Finance and actually hold the handbag?

I saw it with some of my colleagues in the county council who did suffer incredible bows and arrows and did go on. I never really suffered like them. The only time, I think, I ever felt I was being discriminated against was remedied very quickly at an annual meeting of the council. I wanted to be on the executive committee which I thought was one of the top committees. I found out later that it wasn't actually. Our chairman of the county council was a very good man. All councillors constituted the executive and there was nothing that any of us didn't know, so I found the the executive committee never met very much at all. But the only time was when everybody was divvying up the jobs amongst themselves I said to the chap sitting next to me, very nicely, 'Oh I'd really love to be on that committee.' 'Oh don't worry,' he said, 'that's fine, no problem!'

I realized that you only had to ask; in some circumstances I only had to ask. The chair then said, 'Hello—good morning, Councillors and Mrs O'Regan.' I said to him at lunchtime: 'why don't you just call us councillors, it's much easier.' I said, 'I don't like being singled out and yet I'm not a gentleman either.' So he used 'councillors' from that time on, and whenever he'd slip up I'd say, 'Thank you very much, Mr Chairman.' It was always done in good humour. Having a good sense of humour is one of the most important things in political life.

If you can laugh at things and laugh at yourself, that can be the hardest thing.

If you make a mistake and it's a stupid mistake you've got to be able to laugh at yourself. But I value those years in local government. I value the friends I made during that time; and I didn't really suffer the same slings and arrows of discrimination that my other friends did during that time.

Some of the horror stories that you hear about. But either I didn't experience it or I was blind to it and bowled on regardless. Although I look back now and it's a bit like some women who have been working in accountants' firms and places like that and you turn around to them and say, 'Well, don't you ever ask why you're not a partner, or a full partner?'

It's a bit the same I think with me. Why wasn't I elected as an electorate chairman earlier? Why didn't I push myself in that area? I think women have actually got to seize the opportunities themselves, get a good little team of people around them in the party. Work through the party structure and at the same time broaden your interests so that you become a reasonably all-round sort of person with at least a little bit of knowledge. And maybe a concentration on one thing you know well.

And always be pleasant to people. You don't have to grease, but always make sure that you're at meetings, that your name's forward and people start talking about you as a candidate, as somebody who's interested in taking a part in politics. There are always people who are out scouting for women because we do come through different channels. We're not like heads, or chief executives, or even second-tier management in large companies, where perhaps your name is known publicly. And so, unless you're a mayor somewhere, we have to promote ourselves very much on a local basis. Get around to parties and let people know who you are, and even that you are interested in politics. Ruth's probably the best example. She set out to be an MP and she's done all she could possibly do. I don't think she wants to be Prime Minister, I mean what more could you want than to be Minister of Finance and actually hold the handbag?

You have to have a thick skin. Do you know what I mean? The hardening of your heart again. Because if you don't, you fall all over the place mentally and emotionally. But if you harden up a bit then you're accused of not being in touch with people and not knowing what's happening. In actual fact you know damn well what's happening to people and it hurts you to see the pain and suffering that some people have. But it's always been the case. You probably wouldn't be an MP if you didn't have some concern about the human condition and want to actually try and fix it in some way or other.

Ruth Richardson

There are a lot of issues which are common to women on
both sides of the House.

You can look at some of the great behavioural issues like pornography, drink driving, rape law reform. There are a lot of issues which which are common to women on both sides of the House. I worked very closely with Michael Cullen and Fran Wilde on rape law reform. There are many issues that unite parliamentarians, even issues like low inflation. There are some constraints on this economy that don't permit us a wide range of options and there tends to be a coalition—a coalescing of views.

But I think politics is seen as adversarial, and it's in the nature of the reporting of politics that it will emphasize the conflict, not the consensus. But there are many issues where there is common cause—men and women.

8

GENDER POLITICS

Prior to the 1981 election, Parliament was very definitely a male bastion. The new women Members began a process of change which has continued through to the present day. MPs pointed out that most of the men in Parliament have been supportive. Several noted that their male colleagues do not have an easy time either.

Fran Wilde

I tend to use strong language.

There are a lot of great and very civilized male politicians, but they tend not to be the leaders. Geoff [Sir Geoffery Palmer] was a brilliant guy, but he certainly hadn't seen the seamier side of life. He was a constitutional law professor who you felt had been somewhat removed from ordinary life. I think he found women difficult to cope with; very much in the Simone de Beavoir mode of being 'the other'.

If you used a four-letter word in his presence, he found it fairly appalling. I suspect he found it easier if women were pretty and nice and sterile and laughed. If you weren't, that appeared to be very difficult for him. Geoffrey sometimes shouted but I suggest he found it difficult if someone shouted back. I come across very strong. I know that. I tend to use strong language and I do shout and I do swear. Geoffrey would never do that except when he got really stumped for an argument.

The men sometimes bully. I suppose it's not just a male thing. But it tends to be because men have been in positions of power. When they're challenged and they haven't got a rational response then they'll bully. There are a lot of arguments in Cabinet. And there can be some ghastly scenes in Caucus. I've been on the receiving end sometimes. Perhaps it indicates that there are many inadequate people here.

Lange is very good with crowds but not so good one to one. He's brilliant, amazing—a charismatic person. He can't sit down, he's always performing. People who get to know him say he's got ants in his pants. He seems to find it very difficult to sit and concentrate and focus on one person.

I think a lot of political leaders find it difficult to deal with women who

136

are upfront and who might be a bit earthy in how they express themselves. The leadership personality is very interesting. As a trend over time, rather than a basic personality trait, they tend to start believing their own propaganda. They tend to reject advice that's different from what they want. People are always nice to them, and the status of the office tends to overwhelm the reality of the person. I think that's why they get sucked into the propaganda trap.

Sonja Davies

I said, 'Mr Speaker . . . I want you to deal with the
Minister of Police and the Leader of the House.'

I'm the one who says very strongly that half the police force should be women, partly because of sexual abuse. Skilled women constables can deal much better with rape cases, incest cases, because the last thing a woman wants to front up to at a time like that is a fellow. And I believe half of Parliament should be women. I'm not pushing women as women, I'm just saying that as it is at the moment it is not a House of Representatives.

Women have a different perspective to men, and both views are needed. Women are almost half the Norwegian parliament. There are people who say proportional representation will result in that, but I don't believe it will do that at all. You'll get a few more women in, but I'm not interested in that. I think that, once half of the representatives are women, you'll get a system of running Parliament that takes into account women's lives.

People say to me, 'You've been saying you want more women in Parliament but look at Shipley and Richardson.' I say if we had half it wouldn't matter so much. They're both very competent women, I just don't think they happen to live in the real world.

We need more women in Parliament. Because, while there aren't many, you get people like the Member for Titirangi, Marie Hasler, going against the Ministry for Women, querying whether it's necessary and saying sexual harassment is something you have to put up with. She managed, so, so can everybody. That's not a committment to women.

We fought our fight with the men in the Labour Party. There are still pockets there, but there's a lot better attitude to women in this party than there is in the Nats. I think they've still got their battles to come.

When I did get into the House, I was surprised at the sexism and the ageism. John Banks used to call me 'granny' when I was getting up to speak. It never gets into Hansard, because only speeches are recorded.

Hon. Mabel Howard, MP for Christchurch East/Sydenham, 1943–69; Minister of Health, 1947–49; Minister of Social Security, 1957–60. Evening Post

It wasn't until Paul East said, 'Oh God, here's Auntie going to speak' that I just lost my temper. I said, 'Mr Speaker, I want to make a statement. I've put up with ageism and sexism in this House. I want you to deal with the Minister of Police and the Leader of the House.'

The Speaker said he was extremely concerned about it and, you know, they considered what to do about it. Women from the other side came over and thanked me—Katherine O'Regan, Christine Fletcher. I didn't tell my people I was going to do it, I just lost my temper. It welled up and suddenly tipped over.

Then, Muldoon said, 'If you can't stand the heat, girlie, then get out of the kitchen.' And Liz Tennet said, 'Don't you dare call her "girlie" ' Muldoon came over to me and he poked his tongue out. And I said, 'It's dirty, you probably need syrup of figs.'

There are a lot of double standards. Muldoon found it very hard to cope with women at all. My heart just aches for people like the early women MPs. Like Marilyn and before her. When Mabel Howard came in they wouldn't even tell her where the women's toilet was.

It must have been just unbelievable. And then there was the one from Hamilton, Hilda Ross, she was a Cabinet minister. She was there with all these fellows. And it must have been very hard to do that. And Whetu has been in a long time.

Carol Rankin was the first woman Serjeant-at-Arms. She said that when she applied for the job the Speaker asked both Caucuses if they would mind having a woman Serjeant-at-Arms—would they object? She saw it advertised and she applied and eventually got the job. She's given it up now. She's a committee clerk.[1] There have been some changes. We're a long way ahead of Australia, it's even more sexist over there.

I can be naïve. I kept hearing these things about Norman Kirk as I went around as a local body person at meetings—rumours of him and other women. I heard people talking in the hotels about him having relationships. I didn't believe it. I thought he ought to know about these stories and make a big effort to have his wife Ruth up here and be seen with the family.

Of course my husband Charlie said, 'Don't do it, he won't thank you. Trust me, he will not thank you.' And I said, 'Oh no, he's a good friend. I would want him to tell me.' So I was sitting there in his office and I told him. It was just horrendous. I felt like one of those people with one of those bubbles in cartoons, with words coming out of their mouth, I wished I could have stuffed them back. But it was too late.

He stood up, put out his hand and said goodbye. And he never really spoke to me again. I wanted him to say that it's not true, but thanks for telling me, I'll keep an eye out. And I honestly thought he would. Of course, the messenger always gets shot.

Helen Clark

I'm just disgusted at the way politicians behave in proscribing behaviour for other people.

There was a fracas around the Abortion, Sterilisation and Contraception Act. The really bad development was Gerry Wall's private member's bill which as I recall was '74. It was totally opposed by the Labour Women's Council and the Youth Council.

There was very little dialogue on these issues. No one ever could talk to Gerry Wall, I mean he was a very strange man. I'm not sure I ever talked to him in all the years we were in Parliament together. There was a huge generation gap, and a huge belief gap.

When he brought it in, people hadn't been confronted with those issues in a New Zealand Parliament before. And SPUC, this clever organization, went around, it signed up people. It got them identified with it before they knew what the hell they were doing. Of course, once people take a stand like that it becomes very hard to back down. People get sort of locked in.

At the end of the day what the episode showed was that parliamentarians can pass whatever the hell they like and if it's not in accordance with the way people think it should be then it will be totally ignored. That's what happened, people kept having abortions. And citing the mental health of the mother of course means if you're depressed then you get a lawful abortion, and why shouldn't you?

In 1990, as Minister of Health, I brought in an amendment bill to implement two important recommendations of the Abortion Supervisory Committee which had been sitting around. Palmer said he'd do something about them and he just never did. One of my huge frustrations as Minister of Health was picking up things that should have been dealt with in the first year of the Labour Government, not the last, and this was one of them.

The first idea was both to get rid of certifying consultants, who are totally unnecessary and a waste of public money and just build in another barrier. The second was to get rid of the ridiculous age at which people could be told anything about contraception. When the bill was introduced, if we'd been able to deal with it at a reasonable speed, then I think the whole thing would have gone through. There was virtually universal support for the contraception part of it, because time had moved on since Parliament had last discussed it in '77.

AIDS had become a big issue, and people were starting to see that ignorance was actually positively stupid and shouldn't be encouraged, so there was no problem with that part. But the problem is, whenever you put anything into Parliament dealing with that Act, no matter how tightly you try to draft the long and short title of your bill, the fanatics will find a way to expand what your amendment bill does and use that to try and make it worse.

SPUC mounted a huge counter-offensive and got MPs to agree to sponsor amendments to my little bill which was getting rid of certifying consultants. And the amendments would have made counselling compulsory. I've never heard anything so ridiculous—in counselling there has to be a willing party. The sort of counselling services that could have emerged of the Pregnancy Help variety would have been absolutely dreadful.

It started to become a nightmare. As the election got closer, people started to get really twitchy about not losing the support of certain groups in their electorate, I came to the view that if I let the thing go to the committee stage and the third reading we could end up with a worse abortion law than we had before. I've always been very impatient with people who went on and on for six years about how Labour women MPs did nothing to liberalize abortion. We couldn't, the numbers were never there. They're still not there.

Even a little thing like the certifying consultants would have had terrible difficulty getting passed. The chances are that Parliiament would have passed amendments which made the law worse. Each Parliament has got slightly more liberal on moral issues, but it's not liberal enough yet to guarantee safe passage for those kind of things.

I'm just disgusted at the way politicians behave in proscribing behaviour for other people. So, anyway, to cut a long story short, because I believed it was so important to do something on the contraceptive thing because it was holding back effective AIDS education and dealing with teenage sexuality and unwanted pregnancy, I came to the conclusion that the other part of the bill was too risky.

So I put a procedural motion through the House which Government MPs were bound to support and I split the bill. The contraceptive part passed easily and the reason I gave, which was perfectly true, was that at the end of our session there was not enough time to have the proper debate that was needed and it was clear that some people were just going to sit there day and night and debate stupid SPUC-generated amendments.

In the ideal world there'd be no law and the issue would be determined by the woman. I don't agree with consultation with doctors on the decision either, I think that's just silly. I think we're probably forty years off that. But certainly the certifying consultants should be taken out of the bill, because it's just another barrier and a rip-off.

But by and large, if you're only going to tinker you might as well leave the definition of abortion on the grounds of preserving the mental and physical health of the mother because mental health is being quite satisfactorily defined in practice. You don't have to be suicidal. I object to the whole principle of women having to justify their actions to a doctor, and then to two more doctors and then to a surgeon. That's utterly ridiculous.

Getting rid of the restrictive age on contraceptive advice was very important to letting the health education curriculum develop in the schools. It's still not well enough resourced. Things take time to move. It doesn't actually deal head on with the specific issues of sexuality until fairly late. But from the earliest stage in that school health curriculum the emphasis is on positive relationships and self-esteem. The other things kind of naturally grow out of that.

If that could be allowed to work and be properly resourced then I'm quite optimistic, over a ten- or fifteen-year period, of changing a lot of things about this society—linking back to male violence and all the rest of it.

Marie Hasler

Everyone is discriminated against in some way,
including the guys.

I've never really felt there were any obstacles because I was a woman. Once you start feeling that you get rather defensive, you start putting up obstacles. It's more attitude; if you don't see any, there aren't any. I find that's true in the House today. Where people see slights at every turn, I tend to ignore them and barge on.

Everyone is discriminated against in some way, including the guys. I just think you've got to present yourself as you are, take it or leave it. It used to amuse me when I was introduced as a woman candidate. I used to think, 'isn't it obvious?'

Some women were self-conscious but I never thought about it. I just assumed it was normal and natural to be an MP, because once you start thinking it's unusual you're putting yourself into that position. The media and public have always had a preconceived idea of women politicians and how they'd like them to be. If we don't fit into the mould, they say we're trying to act like men. We're not allowed to go outside of that image.

I find a lot of the feminist groups don't really take into consideration that there is a huge diversity of women. We're just as diverse as men, but men aren't expected to act in a prescribed, programmed fashion. They can act however they like and they're not going to get criticized. The feminist movement has had a lot of impact on women's lives in New Zealand. They've done a lot of good in highlighting the things that were very wrong, the injustices, the lack of equal opportunity. But if you ask young women now if they are feminist, I think most would say no. They associate it with a very hard line, dogmatic and somewhat anti-male.

I think the feminist movement has made women look at taking more core subjects at school. It used to be when I was in school—in the ancient past— that you tended to take English and literature and languages. There wasn't as much emphasis on maths and physics and subjects that are really necessary now. You ended up with a BA rather than a BSc. Nowadays I really think you're pretty lucky to get a job with a BA.

Programmed feminists have a very narrow view of what women should be. Women don't want to be strait-jacketed into these ideas. A lot of mainstream women who believe in independence and equal opportunity are not anti-male. They want to get on with men. They want to live with men and share their lives with them. But they don't want to be classified as victims.

Marie Hasler, MP for Titirangi, 1990–.

There are about ten different definitions of feminism, right from the very political lesbian view that women rule the earth. Young women don't want to be feminists because they see it as this strident, slightly lesbian view of the world. So young women haven't got so many role models. I think they need role models that are independent but still feminine, or still as feminine as they want to be, whatever that means. Role models who are independent and can think for themselves.

Feminists tend to want to tell people how to live. There are certain feminist views like the smoke-free legislation that Helen Clark put through, which I think take away the rights of people. I hate smoking, I personally loathe it. But I defend anyone's right to smoke. It isn't an illegal substance, so if we think that it's that bad then we should make it illegal.

Some people are surprised that as a woman I didn't follow gender lines. They tend to think that as a woman you're very health-conscious and you want to tell people they shouldn't smoke. I was told by some of the professional health workers that they were surprised that as a woman I wasn't supporting smoke-free. But as a person I think we're interfering too much. We should encourage people not to smoke. But as a product that people are entitled to sell, you shouldn't stop them advertising it. It's a human right, a civil right.

I hear a lot of women moaning that women can't get into politics. People are prejudiced and it's much harder for us, blah blah. My belief is that we are a conservative society, so we're not going to immediately get women all over the place, but there have been tremendous leaps forward in getting women into responsible positions. I think we've got as many women politicians per capita as most other Western countries. In New Zealand we have produced a Deputy Prime Minister, England's produced a woman Prime Minister, that's pretty good going.

Despite having proportional representation—and I am pro-PR—Europe hasn't produced that. Except in Norway, because they've got an affirmative action policy, a positive discrimination policy in the Labour party there. These are the things people forget. We are conservative and it's going to take a while in terms of putting ourselves up for politics. But women voters aren't in the minority. We're over fifty per cent of the population. So if we can't get women to vote for other women then we've got to look at the reasons why.

I say the first thing is to actually get involved in politics at grass-roots level. Get in there, infiltrate. I don't believe in going into women's groups; rather get into the mainstream of politics. Don't try to get in on women's issues. Get in on everything everyone else is doing or else you're not going to be able to compete. They're going to say you're only interested in a narrow range of issues. I think that's always a danger with so-called women's issues. You've got to be into foreign affairs, trade, all sorts of things, and then you'll be considered a multi-faceted candidate.

Elizabeth Tennet

The female membership of our Parliament is twenty per cent, which is high by world standards, but it's still pathetic.

The Women's Caucus is part of our history. We've always had a women's committee. It's interesting that the National women now have a Caucus committee started in 1990, first time for them. We've had it for yonks.

It's a different perception that the Labour women have. We see ourselves as a collective working for women's issues. We're very proud of having a women's policy, of setting up a women's ministry. We see that there is a role for government to take positive action on women's issues, whereas National

Party women come from a far more individualistic background. They've made it into politics by being as good as any man and see themselves in that role. They've shied away from taking a women's perspective. That's why there's always been that debate in the National Party—of whether they even wanted a Minister of Women's Affairs.

It's a basic difference between a collectivist ethic and an individualistic ethic. That's where the two parties come from and the women very much reflect it. That's why Labour women have always had this strong core of women's issues—fighting for women, seeing women's policy as being something different and being proud of fighting for it. Whereas for National women—their ideology is more that women can become the same as men. It's really up to the woman, they say; if she wants to take up the opportunity then she can. Ruth and Jenny proved it. They have become ministers, and if they can do it then any woman can do it—that's their philosophy.

Labour women are more sympathetic to the view that we need to change structures and provide support mechanisms for women to actually take up these equal opportunities. The female membership of our Parliament is twenty per cent, which is high by world standards, but it's still pathetic. The mere fact of having women in positions of power isn't a saviour in itself—they have to be women that come from a women's perspective and who believe in a caring society.

That again is what separates the Labour women from the National women. Jenny Shipley and Ruth Richardson are two of the most powerful people in the Cabinet, and the decisions that they have taken have impacted on women far more than on men. But I also think some of the hatred against Shipley and Richardson allows a vent for hatred against women. That's part of it. What they've done certainly deserves a lot of dislike, but they have received more because they've been women.

Judith Tizard

. . . I certainly agree with Susan Faludi that the problem is not feminism, but that feminism has not been tried.

There's a strong sense of camaraderie amongst women in the Labour Party. We tend to have worked together for many years and we know each other quite well. We tend to give each other a lot of support.

There's a much greater range of views, I think in the National Party. Chris Fletcher, I think, would see herself as a liberal. There are a number of issues that she has sought to work with us on. Then there's somebody like Gail

Gail McIntosh, MP for Lyttelton, 1990–. Photos by Woolf, Wellington

McIntosh who makes the most extraordinary speeches which make you wonder if she has ever thought what life is like for people who have not had access to education or haven't had happy marriages. I knew Ruth Richardson slightly in WEL in Wellington when it was first set up. I found her views absolutely alien then.

At about the same time I became involved in party politics I became involved in student politics and women's organizations, and I basically discovered that I had no more in common with a lot of Tory women than I did with a lot of Tory men. I had much more in common with men of the Labour Party and some men of the union movement. It's a matter of attitude and outlook, rather than a sexual line. But I do think many women have a different way of looking at the world.

So there are some things I can work with them on. For example, when Sonja Davies was being abused by some of the National Members in the House, several of the National women came over and said, 'Thank you for sticking up for yourself on that one. You should hear the sort of thing we have to put up with.'

The level of sexist language and ageist language was something with which we do not have to deal in the Labour Party. I mean we've sensitized people enough to language, even if we haven't changed their attitudes. There's no way someone in the Labour Party would say, 'Go on, Granny, have a go' as John Banks regularly used to. I was quite stunned. If they're putting up with that sort of stuff—why? You just have to say 'stop' and make it really clear.

Jim Bolger's stupid comments about Joan Kirner are indicative of the mindset.[2] If you get away with that sort of nonsense with the people you work with, then presumably you say it in public and you embarrass yourself.

We're dealing with a total reversal of the sort of social contract New Zealand has had since about 1949, and I will not work with the betrayers. Those women who are supporting the sorts of policies the National Government is pursuing in housing, in education, in health. All of those are basic things about how women look after their children, about women's power to get out of a violent marriage or a violent relationship; those things are so fundamental to me, and I see those women as condoning the increasing inequality.

It's interesting that women who don't describe themselves as feminists see issues like that as feminist issues. But women and men who do describe themselves as feminists see those as social issues, they see it as part of the whole picture.

Women have to take responsibility for their children, we have no choice. And I know no women who have had a child who have not, one way or another, felt that their whole life has changed. I know some men who have had children and it's barely made a ripple in their lives. At that point you have to say, what are the social structures that have developed? It seems to me you've got to perpetuate the good ones and try to get rid of the bad ones, and if that makes me a feminist, I can only quote Rebecca West: 'people call me a feminist whenever I express sentiments that differentiate me from a doormat.'

I am not prepared to have someone say to me, 'Good housing policy is feminist, therefore I reject it.' What a load of garbage. Good housing policy is about human beings not having to worry themselves sick to keep a roof over their heads, so that they can think about getting their kids an education, getting health care, all the things that make life possible. So I see it as a cohesive whole.

We would all be better off if we spent more time looking at long-term social accounting as well as economic accounting. What you don't spend in an area in human resources or in money, you pay for later, and if Society would rather pay for prisons than child care then I think that choice has got to be made really clearly rather than by default.

Because of the nature of politics, policy makers tend to see things in terms of three-year blocks. They tend to look at the short-term savings instead of long-term gain.

Most New Zealanders have a fairly strong feeling of fairness, so I have no embarrassment or concern about expressing those ideas, just as I have no concern about being identified as a feminist. I feel very strongly that I have the right to speak and I will go on saying it. And I'm delighted at the constant feedback I get. People will often come up after a meeting that we've had a less than warm response to and say: 'Thank you for saying that. I feel really strongly about that but I've always been embarrassed expressing it.' I remember coming home very upset from school because someone had been very rude about my father, and he said, 'You've got to know that even in a good election only about half the people will vote for us. You've got to assume that half the bastards are against us to start with.'

The instinct for politicians is that they need to be liked, they need votes,

Judith Tizard, MP for Panmure, 1990–, with her mother, Dame Catherine Tizard.
Ernie Gilgen

they need support; but then you've also got to have the courage to say honestly what you think and discuss ideas.

It would be paralysing if people just said yes every time you opened your mouth, and didn't tell you what was wrong. Unless I am prepared to clearly explain my ideas, my views, I'm not going to get to what people feel comfortable with; but I hope I'm also giving people more ingredients for their views too.

There is going to be a reaction to every perceived change, I think that's what we're going through with the Waitangi Tribunal. The perception is that somehow or other the Māori tribes have got too much, so people say, 'We've got to take the power to get that back.'

Feminism is certainly being blamed for changes which I think were coming anyway. Why would women who have education accept half the pay of their male contemporaries? We're talking about basic equity issues. Why should women accept worse housing, economic insecurity in marriage, lack of access to health services. Really basic stuff. So I certainly agree with Susan Faludi that the problem is not feminism, but that feminism has not been tried.

It brings you back to the arguments put up about Christianity. That Christianity hasn't worked. It hasn't been tried, and my view is that Christianity probably would be very feminist in its basic form. There are things like human rights and human needs that have to be recognized which are basic to our operation and participation as human beings in society.

Margaret Austin

. . . I moved into his territory in a way teachers can if they're using their power.

Comments were made about Labour women. There were snide comments in debate, and sometimes when people were passing in the corridors of the House. Some of the younger ones got really upset by the innuendo, so I said to them, 'Leave it to me, see how we go.'

I picked up a notebook. The very first person to make a really sexist remark was Merv Wellington. I wrote down what he said and got up out of my seat and went straight over to him. I said, 'Did you say this?'—'Yes.'— 'To whom was it directed? Was it so and so?' At that point he got all embarrassed. I said, 'Thank you, you have verified it.' I did that a couple more times to the others and virtually the whole thing dried up.

One other person who I baled up one night was John Banks. That was in the dining room of Bellamy's. He made these comments over supper. I just eyeballed him. I got so incensed I moved into his territory in a way teachers can if they're using their power. He had made personal comments to me and I just went straight in. I can't remember what I said now, but I was in full flight and gave him a dressing-down and said I wasn't prepared to put up with that sort of nonsense.

Later on when I became Whip in 1988 comments were made against Annette King and Anne Collins. There had been some innuendo made in their direction. I thought I'll prepare myself with both Standing Orders and Speakers' Rulings and the very first opportunity I get I will ask the Speaker and invoke his protection.

I just waited for the opportunity for something to come across the House and it did on this day. I acted straight away. I had the speech all prepared, I had the page references for both Standing Orders and Speakers' Rulings and I invoked them and called upon the Speaker to protect these women.

Judy Keall

Compared with men who had been in a profession, perhaps, and had been able to be reasonably single-minded about it, we did have an advantage.

It never really hit me until that first Tuesday morning when I went out to Auckland airport to get the early plane to Wellington. It was in the days before they had those covered ways. I looked out across the tarmac and there was this long line of men in business suits, reaching as far as I could see. I guess there might have been one or two other women, but I felt as if I was the only one. That was when it really hit me actually, that I was going into the male-dominated world.

Anne Collins and I shared a bench together in the first few years, and very soon after we'd started one of the men on our side was complaining, 'Oh, you're supposed to do so many things all at once. Here we are, we're expected to listen to the debates, prepare a speech, process our correspondence all at the same time.' Anne said something like, 'Stop your whingeing. We're used to cooking a meal, answering the phone, helping our kids with their homework, preparing the shopping-list, feeding the baby all at the same time.' She said, 'I'd much rather be doing this.'

I can remember thinking, yes, we were actually adapting better than the men because we had that flexibility. We are more used to the concept of doing a thousand and one things all at once. Compared with men who had been in a profession, perhaps, and had been able to be reasonably single-minded about it, we did have an advantage.

The biggest shock I had was when I went to a parliamentary conference in Darwin in 1987 and realized how far behind New Zealand the Australian men were. Their MPs were a pack of chauvinists compared to ours. I realized that, despite all our complaints about a male-dominated work area, we were much better off than the women in Australia were. Much more careful about our language too. It really hit me.

Christine Fletcher

*. . . that contributed quite significantly in terms of me
actually seeking political representation. Because to me
if there is one time in your life when you are vulnerable
it's when you're lying with your legs apart trying
to push a baby out . . . .*

One of the strongest motivations in an overtly political sense was the birth of my daughter Jean.

I had no choice in where she was born, and she was actually born in a corridor because National Women's was full at the time. I became involved with a group of midwives trying to get an alternative maternity centre off the ground, where we lost the fight but won the war. I mean the developer that we wanted backed out and different things happened, but the enormous sense of frustration at dealing with bureaucracy and trying in terms of women's health to raise the status in terms of providing choice.

It was back when Helen Clark was Minister of Health—she did a good job in terms of the midwifery legislation that empowered midwives. But there was no way in which the area health boards were prepared to contract out to alternative community-based non-high-tech-type care.

And that was a major battle, that contributed quite significantly in terms of me actually seeking political representation. Because to me if there is one time in your life when you are vulnerable it's when you're lying with your legs apart trying to push a baby out and you're in the middle of a corridor and fifty people are watching you and saying, 'How are you feeling, are you alright?'

I had no choice over my environment because with my first child there had been some complications. I wasn't allowed to have a home birth. Boy, that peeved me off. But those midwives are wonderful. I mean they have fought the battle against the male establishment and they are winning.

Katherine O'Regan

The longer I am involved in politics the more I realize that perhaps this caring, nurturing bit about women is a bit of a myth.

When I first went in I found sitting in the Chamber an overpowering feeling. The only women around were the Hansard women and the occasional senior management person from the Department who sat up by the Speaker during the Estimates debate. Otherwise it was terribly overpowering. You couldn't escape it.

I vaguely recall the time I was a county councillor and attending a county conference in Dunedin or somewhere. There were only four women out of 400 or 600 county councillors. I reached the stage where I couldn't stand it. I had to escape to a women's hairdresser. I don't go to hairdressers very often, but it was just for a bit of female companionship. I'd never experienced that before, so I can understand why Marilyn used to say that it was very lonely, because she was the only [National] woman for three years.

When there are 'women's issues' it's always interesting. On most women's issues, violence or whatever, the women will always support one another. We may differ on ways and means, but we would support the views of one another.

But I learnt very early on that there was no way that the two sides of the House could meet. There was only Ruth Richardson and I on our side for the first three years. I didn't really know the place and so I suggested to Margaret Shields one day that perhaps we could meet as a group of parliamentary women. I was at that early stage where I was thinking, 'Let's try and all muck in together.' She very gently informed me that she thought it would be most unwise. I was quite hurt at the time.

Now I can understand why. I'd say the same to a new Member. There are some issues that women can meet on, but the philosophical barriers are actually too great. That's how it should be I think, in our type of system. That's why I don't think you'll ever see a women's party. In the end there'll be women with different philosophical views and you won't have that unity that's required.

The old building gave you a greater feeling of maleness which isn't quite so present in the temporary place. The wood panelling and the high ceiling and the big leather chairs in the lounges, and one imagines Dick Seddon reclining there with a cigar.

The place we're in at the moment, it's temporary thank heavens, is like being in a formica room. And the ceiling is low. You can hear everything.

You can see the whites of the eyes across the alley. It's not quite so impersonal, and you get far more fractious behaviour when it becomes too personal.

Unfortunately the men don't always seem to realize when they are being offensive. Some things do hurt and they do hurt women particularly. Helen Clark has an awful lot flung at her because of the severe haircut and the sort of clothes which give her a cold demeanour. But she's a very intelligent women. Politically we're poles apart, but I admire her. Another person I admire is Fran Wilde—what a gutsy woman—as I say, poles apart politically. Sonja Davies has given wonderful service to this country in child care and in the union movement. Those women really are just marvellous.

I look at Sue Wood and I think, 'My God, she should really be in the House.' We've wasted her talents and the country is the poorer for not having her here.

The longer I am involved in politics the more I realize that perhaps this caring, nurturing bit about women is a bit of a myth. There is viciousness in women. Okay, we do have the babies and by and large we do the caring and we concern ourselves about the state of the planet. But why, then, as the carers and nurturers, have we allowed sexual abuse to continue and sometimes participate in physical abuse? Why, then, do we, if we're supposed to care for the planet, continue to buy goods which are damaging to the planet?

Why aren't we more prudent and careful in expenditure in the home instead of being wasteful and throwing away food and goods and clothing that we don't need any more? So where's the caring and the nurturing? Maybe we've come to believe the advertising and the propaganda. By nature women have to be the more caring or nurturing ones because they're the ones who are given the job of mothering the children, I don't think it always works out that way. I think that there are many men who, if given the chance, would have the same feelings.

We say women are the only ones who can care and nurture, and we are still the ones who are beating up on our kids and neglecting them. Sometimes you can be criticized for being anti-women for saying those things. But it has to be said sometimes. We were just doing Women's Refuge Week this week and it's focused on male violence. It's true, most of it is male violence, but we also know that women who have been brutalized can also brutalize. It's up to us to try and stop that. It's not as easy as it sounds.

I'm fortunate enough to come from an environment where no one raised their voices, let alone their hands. I've never been able to understand that people can actually live in a violent relationship and be happy. I don't think you could possibly be. It's a contradiction in terms.

Margaret Shields

I don't think that we will have really made a difference until we have enough women going into politics to form a critical mass.

In my maiden speech I said it was not enough for women to get in. The values associated with women like compassion must also get into power. Not the Margaret Thatchers who are women but think the same way as men.

I don't think that we will have really made a difference until we have enough women going into politics to form a critical mass. I think there's really only one country in the world that's done that so far, and that's Norway where it's forty per cent.

I don't think it's too far off here because I think that New Zealand has been going along the only path that leads to stable change. Particularly in the Labour Party there has been a steady increase in the involvement of women in the party as activists, not just as support staff. That's very important. If you look around the world you will find that there are women who have been Prime Ministers of countries but without that kind of grass-roots support, without those different levels of activity.

You might have a woman Prime Minister but once she's gone, that's it. And in many of the countries that have had women in high office they have been there not because of changes in gender relations, but because they happened to belong to élites.

It's changed enormously in New Zealand. I remember a group of women going to see Norman Kirk. We were campaigning for the Women's Council of the Labour Party. And he told us in so many words that he really didn't need a stronger Women's Council, he had a wife to advise him.

I think he was worried about a political backlash, and he did not see it as important. I didn't know until after he had died that he was very supportive of my taking a candidacy. He certainly never indicated that to me. I think he found it quite difficult at times to relate to stroppy women. And I must have seemed like a pretty stroppy woman at the time.

As far as I'm concerned feminism means standing up for women. If you can't stand up for your own sex, you can hardly expect men to support you. Often you would go out to a group and you would find people saying, 'Well, I'm not really a feminist, we're not really feminists.'

I found with women that the only way to approach that question was to say, 'Are you sure?' And they'd sort of look slightly bewildered and that would be an opening to explain, 'By feminism, what I mean is so and so and so and so.' And they'd say, 'Oh, yes, well I agree with that.' And I'd say, 'Well, you mightn't know it but you're a feminist, and that's good.'

Notes

1.   Carol Rankin is the author of *Women and Parliament 1893–1993. 100 Years of Institutional Change.* (Wellington: Office of the Clerk of the House of Representatives, 1993.) Significantly enough, Ms Rankin's monograph contains a section (pp. 34–36) entitled, 'Plumbing' in which she notes that, as recently as 1984, Anne Collin's action in physically relabelling a set of men's toilets 'unisex' met with opposition from a number of male MPs.
2.   In August 1992, Prime Minister Jim Bolger attracted widespread criticism for applying the adage, 'The show's not over 'til the fat lady sings' to Joan Kirner, Premier of Victoria.

9

MEDIA

A thick skin and a sense of humour were the qualities most often cited by MPs as requirements for dealing with the news media.

The relationship is a complex one: MPs cannot get by without the media, and the reverse is equally true. A politician's success is often measured by the coverage they receive. Nevertheless, no matter how much experience an MP has, they can never completely distance themselves emotionally from criticism, whether deserved or otherwise.

Marilyn Waring

The media is a consumption item. Who has the most disposable cash to buy it? Boys. So who's your customer and who do you have to please? Boys.

I don't approve of most of what Richardson and Shipley are doing, but if John Banks was Minister of Social Welfare and Doug Kidd was Minister of Finance we wouldn't have anything like that attention.

If women were in charge of the editorial pages, the front page, and the economics page and business pages it might change. But they're not.

It's just a question of process too. Again, since 1975 there have been enormous changes. There wasn't a woman editor of a major paper and there has been in several instances since then. Judy Addinall from the *New Zealand Herald* was the only woman in the press gallery when I arrived in 1976. So time is going to take care of some of those things.

But again you come back to the question, what is the media? The media is a consumption item. Who has the most disposable cash to buy it? Boys. So who's your customer and who do you have to please? Boys. It's part of the market reality. I can't go around banging my head against the wall because the media isn't an information or an educative channel—it wasn't born and bred to be. It's there to sell papers or sell advertising. Boys have the purse strings where that's concerned.

What's news? *Good Morning New Zealand* is news. Television New Zealand is not. It's entertainment—info-tainment. Whatever you like to call

Marilyn Waring with former US Congresswoman, Bella Abzug, April 1988.
Waikato Times

it, it's not news. Newspapers are a five-minute consumption exercise for tomorrow's fish and chip papers.

I'm interested in information. I'm interested in research activity. Then I'm interested in making up my own mind. I'm not interested in propagandistic nonsense. It's not news to me; it's propaganda.

When I stay in the room long enough to watch it, I find myself talking back to the TV news. Now that these long summer evenings are here on the farm, I seldom watch.

But I do think for women politicians the New Zealand news media are a cinch. I mean you just don't have to spend any money on advertising. You can use them like puppets and I did. Particularly, in those days, if you were only one or one of two in Government. It was just so simple.

For example, when we found out twenty-four hours beforehand that

Doug Kidd was going to drop his Abortion bill in 1984, I literally used Radio New Zealand in the evening and *Morning Report* to get the strategy and tactics out. Once I was live on air, I just went for it.

This is what has to be done now. Too bad about the questioner. It's the same with TV soundbites. If you only want a twenty-second message to get across it doesn't matter what they ask you; just say that phrase again and again and again. They've driven that many miles to get you, that's all they've got in the finish. They've gotta use it. It's really simple.

Helen Clark

. . . it's just a different kind of poison from what would be applied to male politicians.

There was a smear campaign over smoke-free, that's irrefutable. I actually spoke to someone in the public relations company that had the tobacco account. She told me that the campaign was geared at whipping up hatred against me as a person, except they didn't expect the death threats. People rang in saying they'd like to kill me and that sort of thing.

They went for my jugular. The person I spoke to was taking the line that, if I didn't back off, it would finish me off politically. That was their objective. The public relations campaign was very personal. They tried to break me but it didn't work.

Smoke-free put New Zealand in the forefront of health promotions. Which one always knew it would.

If they do move against it, when I'm Minister of Health again I will move to repeal their repeal. End of story. It just seems like an anachronism, having had such success in weaning sport and culture off tobacco, to let it happen again.

Professionally, as a politician, you have to watch the news, I don't get any information from it whatsoever. But you have to flip it on, you record it and flash it through because you have to see what people are seeing.

It's the same with the press. Again, you learn very little from the press because you're part of the news, you're one of the newsmakers. But you monitor. Some things are cut out of the diet, I don't read *Metro* any more. Why subject yourself to that? *North and South*, the same category. I get tired of magazines that are proprietorily driven, driven by New Righters, who employ left-wing political columnists who try to kick the hell out of you. If they can't get you on the Right they'll get you on the Left.

I have a lot of respect for independent journalists, people who are hard reporters but are also fair reporters. Columnists who have affiliations should be identified. Strong partisan columns are fine, as long as people don't cover up where they're coming from. Life's difficult enough without exposing myself to that sort of rubbish. There are a few more women journalists these days. It is better. But for the most part they're not the senior people.

You develop a pretty thick skin. Most people don't have to put up with the hammering that politicians take. Look at Bolger, he's like blotting paper. He's been punched so often he's dizzy. And one of National's problems in even thinking about changing leaders is that they all know that probably no one could have stood up to it better. Doug Graham could not have stood up to what Bolger stood up to. I'm not saying that makes Bolger any good, but he's been hammered and hammered. In the end it gets to people.

David Lange took a terrible pounding. He resigned. The tide just went over. He went from being the darling to being the media's punching-bag. He could have won a confidence motion but it would have been narrow. By that time it would have been a Pyrrhic victory because there'll be another one. Other politicians cut away the foundations, but the media played its part in his downfall, no doubt about that. They're hunting a quarry. Their greatest satisfaction can come from cutting someone down and then moving on to the next target.

I don't think it's very different for women. There is a difference in the kind of criticism. Once they decide to go for you they go in ways they wouldn't go for men. So they'll go for your clothes and your haircut and that sort of silly stuff. But in the end I'm not sure it's more poisonous, it's just a different kind of poison from what would be applied to male politicians. It's cyclical. Comes and goes, comes and goes.

Ruth Richardson

If the criticism is invalid it's like a rubber bullet, it bounces off.

The media like anybody else tend to indulge in stereotyping. Jenny Shipley and I have been given twin responsibilities that have called for a good deal of action and initiative. But it's like the law of physics. The law of action will be met with the law of reaction. That doesn't surprise us. We're both pretty level-headed, we understand the nature of the responsibilities that we have been asked to assume. We're both very settled family people and that helps enormously in handling the pressure.

I find that as long as you've got your head and your heart in the right place, as long as you know what you stand for, if there's valid criticism take it on board. If the criticism is invalid it's like a rubber bullet, it bounces off.

They write about the way women look but that's part of the stereotype. Women are noticed more and that's just a fact of life. The journalists tend to apply a different standard to a woman and to a man. In my view that's a reflection on men and I don't let it trouble me. If somebody is prejudiced that's their problem, not mine. My own personal motto has been that performance will always prevail over prejudice. Sometimes you've just got to be a bit patient.

Margaret Moir

It's taken me at least a year and a bit to . . . be able to get myself at arm's length from some of the criticism.

Many women—and I am certainly in this bracket—tend to take criticism very personally. It's taken me at least a year and a bit to work through that, and be able to get myself at arm's length from some of the criticism. You have to be aware of the criticism and be able to take on board messages that you're being given, but I've been very hurt by some of the public criticism in the media, especially my local media.

There were reports that were made, especially by the Labour Party in the first year, that I found that quite hard to take. Reports that you don't work hard, that you're not doing your job. Letters to the editor I find quite difficult too. But you've got to think, 'Hey, is that criticism justified?' If it is, think, 'Well, how can I take that on board and make sure that I understand the message that I'm being given?'

There are compensations. I've had high points where I've been able to help people or I've received a message or card, a bunch of flowers, or a box of chocolates, or just a phone call to say, 'Hey, thanks.' I really do value that little indication from someone that you have helped them. Whether or not they've got exactly what they've wanted, they've appreciated the help you've given them.

There's another level. My husband and I were overseas last year in March for a Commonwealth Parliamentary Association seminar and we met both the Queen and John Major and I thought, 'Hey, is this for real?' We had a service in Westminster Abbey that same visit. The Commonwealth countries were participating and it was a very moving experience, in Westminster Abbey with the full choir and the New Zealand flag going past us.

Anne Collins

Muldoon said something about how I'd deserted my children.

There was a huge story in one of the weekly papers—the *Sunday News*—accusing me of being on holiday when I should have been attending to this industrial crisis in my electorate.

It was an interesting story because I'd have never been invited and, even if I had, I never would have gone near the place. Because no one would ever want an MP present at a stopwork matter. That is not the way industrial relations work. You do not have political grandstanders when you're trying to sort out a dispute.

They actually got hold of me down the West Coast, with my family. We'd been to a Labour Party conference in Christchurch and we took a few days off on the West Coast before we came home. We hadn't had any time together for ages. The children would have been four and eight, or something like that. It did quite a good job for my profile in the electorate. I saw the story when I was on my way home, it was at Wellington airport.

I couldn't believe it. Front-page stuff. It was just amazing. I mean if I'd been absent when the earthquake was on, or straight after Cyclone Bola yeah, I should have been there. I should have been working for the people and making representations to the government and all that sort of stuff that I did. I could have sympathized. But a stopwork meeting at the mill? It's just bizarre.

I made some of that worse for myself, because on this one occasion when they got hold of me and complained that my electorate secretary wouldn't let them know where I was I said, 'I'll buy her a box of chocolates.' So I shouldn't have been such a smart-ass.

I don't think you can protect yourself from everything. It could have been worse. They could have done front-page stuff with my marriage breakup. That would have been really mucky. When you consider what happened to David Lange or Kerry Burke. The only difference was that nobody had given anybody a story on ours. If they'd got someone to talk . . .

There was a guy who kept writing threatening letters. This editor said, 'If you don't deny this I'll take it and I'll print it.' It was a story that I had deserted my children and run off with a Cabinet minister. And I just kept saying, 'No comment, no comment.'

That was the story that he wanted to print. It was a Sunday paper. They rang Bryce, my ex-husband, on a Friday afternoon, about three o'clock to see if they could get something out of him. I was there, looking after Evan because he'd come home from a school camp. I used to pick up the children on Friday afternoons and have them for the weekend, but Bryce and I had organized that I'd be there early that time because Evan was coming home early.

They couldn't work out why I was at home, because they said things like, 'Is that Anne Fraser? Is that Anne Fraser, the MP?' and I said, 'Yes, yes.'[1] And they'd asked to speak to Bryce and I said, 'No, he hasn't come home yet.' And I think that sort of threw them a bit. But if anyone had talked, they would have gone for it. There would have been a lot more substance to that story than the other rubbish.

Muldoon did a story about me. It must have been in a Sunday paper; about me when I went to an International Parliamentary Union conference in London and Michael organized his ministerial trip to coincide so that we'd have some time together while we were both away. It was right before Mike and I got married.

Muldoon said something about how I'd deserted my children. He said this in print, because I got a letter from a woman in Cambridge. She'd written to me to say how dastardly it was that I'd deserted my kids. But in fact I'd taken my son with me. So I wrote this very nice letter back to her and said, 'No, no, I haven't deserted my children, one of them came with me and we had a wonderful time.' I didn't even know that Muldoon had done it till she wrote. But then she wrote back and apologized, which was rather nice. It's hard work—all the expectations, the negative feedback. I hardly ever got any positive feedback. I felt that I became really boring, all I could do was talk about politics, that's all I had time for.

Lianne Dalziel

You do all that work and you just get cheated.

It's important to have that debating chamber where the public can come and watch, and that it's heard on the radio. I think it would be better if they allowed more television screening. They have more rights to televise than they ever had before and they hardly use them.

Just a couple of weeks ago the television cameras turned up out of the blue in the middle of oral questions. I thought it was odd, but then Winston Peters walked in, sat down at his desk, shuffled a few papers, and they filmed him. Then he got up and walked out. And then the cameras went away again. So it was all just jacked up.

Judith Tizard on election night, 1987.

I've still heard people saying, 'Why didn't you object to the ACC changes?' That's the thing I hate the most, that you battle away in the privacy of the select committee. The media don't give us very good coverage on the select committees.

I don't know how many meetings on ACC I had around the country, but I held a briefing session for the journalists in the gallery because they just weren't running any stories on it. They couldn't get their heads around the fact that this bill represented a massive change, and they all bought Birch's publicity, which was: ACC is here to stay, it's business as usual. It's really hard to get across to the media what changes are being proposed and, since they don't come to the select committees, they don't know.

The one that annoyed me the most was the person who stood for Wellington Central, Denis Welch. He did come to my briefing but he left ten minutes after I started to explain what the changes were really going to mean. Then he wrote a scathing article, attacking us for our former ACC policy. He didn't mention my name once and said that the Opposition had done nothing to oppose measures Birch brought in. It put me off him. He's really been an Alliance sympathizer all the time. Now that he's come out, as it were, people know where he stood. But it's just bloody annoying. You do all that work and you just get cheated like that. That was political, that wasn't really being ignored, that was being deliberately ignored. But I do get a lot of news media coverage really, for a minor, new Opposition back-bencher.

Katherine O'Regan

Your defences drop. It's like an egg really, that the shell comes off. You're fairly tender and vulnerable.

Sometimes the press can be nasty, other times they can be very nice as well. I was described on TV as being the only nice person in the House. I guess I was quite pleased that I could be thought of as being a nice person. Maybe that's a fault in a way, in that, if you're nice, you never get things done. But, as I said to my staff the other day, I don't think I have the animal instinct, the instinct, to go in for the kill.

Everyone makes mistakes. There was the issue of trying to live for a week on the benefit. That was actually about eating healthily on a certain amount. I wasn't in the best of health. I was in the throes of having major surgery and it was stupid; I really should have known better.

I was launching nutrition guidelines, and in the body of the book it suggested a certain menu and then the cost, and I thought it was quite expensive and I said, 'I'm sure I could could eat cheaper than that but still eat healthily and eat well.'

It sort of grew from there. I'm not sure I ever really said, 'I will go on the benefit', but I think I said something that sounded like it. That, if I was on a benefit, I was sure I could cope, which then turned into: 'I'm going on the benefit.' I regret saying it and I guess for many people it was just a bit too much, and I'm still receiving very anti letters occasionally, from different people. You know, 'It's a year since you said blah blah blah.'

But I'll tell you what has happened from that. There has been a lot of publicity on cheapies from supermarkets, cheap recipes, how to live on forty dollars a week and live healthily. And so I'd like to think that that action of mine perhaps was the catalyst for organizations to get up and do something for women who are trying to live on a smaller budget. The Country Women's Institutes and local polytechs—all sorts of organizations are beginning to take up that challenge. But, I probably deserved that. I was dumped upon, although I did it all for the right reasons.

You need a sense of humour. My husband and I had just had our honeymoon. We were married earlier but we'd just had our honeymoon. We were a week away with no radios, no television, absolutely nothing. Just books and sun and sea and each other. It was very, very pleasant.

Your defences drop. It's like an egg really, that the shell comes off. You're fairly tender and vulnerable. I came back and read an article that rated New Zealand politicians in the Sunday paper. And I was actually four on the list of five of the lowest on your scorecard. I felt quite vulnerable and terribly hurt by that.

Although it's a junky journalist having a poke at politicians, no matter what anybody said, it hurts. You should say, 'This is a load of nonsense, don't take any notice of it.' But you do take notice of it and it hurts. Muldoon used to say, 'If it's too hot in the kitchen get out.' Then you say to them, 'No, I'm not going to be beaten by that.'

But it's always been the case. You probably wouldn't be a Member of Parliament if you didn't have some concern about the human condition and want to actually try and fix it in some way or other. So when I came back and read that in the paper of course it hurt.

If you start looking at the cartoons about the women, you'll find that they're much harsher and more sexist in their approach than they are with men. Especially like Jenny Shipley and Ruth. Jenny's been portrayed as the sort of Gestapo concentration camp woman. They've portrayed Ruth as Madame Lash. Michael Cullen called her Madame Lash in the House which I find quite disgusting. He wouldn't say that of Helen Clark, I'm sure—he'd soon get a whip around the ears if he did!

It would be worthwhile looking at those cartoons and comparing them with other Ministers of Finance. There's a sex thing in there. A Minister of Finance portrayed as a Gestapo bloke with a whip in his hand doesn't carry the same message as a woman. A woman conjures up bondage and masochism and all that, which is far heavier than that which a man might carry.

I watched TV last night, about why women read Mills and Boons. I didn't realize we had some women millionaires in New Zealand who write Mills and Boons stories, I couldn't believe it. But it was interesting. I'm not sure that the hardline feminists would agree, but there are some feminists who are saying that these are actually really sexy books to read. Obviously I hadn't read any for years—in fact I can't ever recall reading one—all a bit soft and pappy for me. But they were putting forward the view that they are women-centred. Books that are written, particularly by men, are more male-centred, whereas in these it was the women that were the heroes or heroines, and that's the difference in connotation too. It's the women's experience and not male experience which made them an interesting study for feminists who were looking at women's literature. I thought, 'Good lord, all of a sudden Mills and Boons have become respectable.' I was quite amused. But I can understand what they mean about the women-centredness of the books. I find that quite interesting.

Note

1.   'Anne Fraser' was the married name under which Ms Collins was elected to Parliament.

10

THE NEW REALITY

The pace of change in New Zealand has not lessened in the nineties. Major social developments and market realignments have been politically driven, and the debate on future directions is growing rather than subsiding. There is clearly no going back. But, just as clearly, the choices have not yet been settled.

Ruth Richardson

> *. . . positions aren't worth everything. Principles are very important.*

You've got to be willing to break the mould. And there are many women in Parliament who have broken the mould. Politics is a brilliant career in the sense that it's what you want to make it. There are some constraints, and you've got to work within other people's expectations, and sometimes myths and prejudices, and that's a blight on the existence. But for all that, it's what you want to make it. I've never known any women who have been willing to accept imposed boundaries. Sometimes there will be self-imposed boundaries.

Women are more fearless than men. Women basically don't owe anything to the *status quo*, because the *status quo* has generally been adverse to women, has generally loaded the dice against women. So women to get there have had to break a lot of moulds, have had to challenge a lot of settled views. For my part, every minute counts. At the end of the day I think women tend to be surer about their bottom lines and politics, and positions aren't worth everything. Principles are very important.

Helen Clark

> *. . . once you kill off hope you can't really be surprised that crime soars and people kill themselves.*

My priorities when Labour gets back in are to remove the commercialization of the health system and to bring back publicly accountable boards with decision-making power. In fact, to decentralize health decision making again. Because the system that is being set up is incredibly ministerially driven. Ministers appoint every decision maker at every board. There is no accountability back to the public. I think that's wrong.

With housing, again, I think you have to decommercialize Housing New Zealand. It has to go back to looking something like the Housing Corporation did, where it allocates houses to people on the basis of need and charges a rent that they can afford.

We no longer have social housing in New Zealand. If you can't pay the rent of the so-called State house, you don't get into it. There's no rational system of queuing for State housing like there used to be, with the result being that the emergency houses are closing. When there's no rational allocation mechanism on the grounds of need, there's no point in people going and waiting in an emergency house because there's nothing to wait for. They can't pay the rent of the state house even if they get one. So de-commercialization in the social sector is going to be top priority.

We'll be paying more for health care costs by the damage done to people's health from falling income, unemployment, poor housing, and so on. We're paying more for the jails and law enforcement. We're not going to be able to solve those problems by throwing more money at health, either. There are studies that show that widening the distribution of income has a direct effect on life expectancy. In Britian, when income differentials widened greatly in the early Thatcher period, life expectancy actually fell. I suspect that is happening in New Zealand, but we don't have the information, we don't have the data to even attempt to measure that.

New Zealand has such a high youth suicide rate because young people have got little to hope for. A few years ago young people felt very despondent about the prospect of nuclear war. They had every reason to be, when Reagan and Brezhnev were squaring off. Now I think it's become very personal, because a lot of them are in families which have experienced unemployment and they're at schools where people come back year after year because there's no job to go to. I think it's directly related to socio-economic policies that they're part of. They can't see any hope, and that's a terrible thing.

It breaks your heart to go to a high-school prize-giving in poorer areas of Auckland and see these really lovely kids. Then you look at how many kids from last year's graduation actually got a job or went on to a polytech and it can be pitifully low. There are students coming back for an eighth form. Who wants to go back for an eighth form? You only go back because there's nowhere else to go.

I suspect that, because times have been so hard, there's a feeling of fatalism about the point of it anyway. We've kind of succeeded in killing off hope, and once you kill off hope you can't really be surprised that crime soars and people kill themselves. Because what are you giving them to live for?

When you and I left school we never for a moment expected we would be unemployed. You walked into the job of your choice. In some parts of Auckland now kids will still walk into the job of their choice because they're well connected. They're going to get into the medical school, they're going to go through the law school, they're going to get there. But the kids who are battling it up from lower-income homes have no such reason to feel optimistic. A lot of them are going to try, but there's a significant proportion who aren't making it.

One of the answers has to be stimulating economic growth. In the end that's the only thing that's going to restore opportunity to people with or without education. Places of further education and training just have to keep on increasing to try to pick up the numbers who want to be part of it. I have general faith that in the end people with skills and qualifications are going to make it. But it needs that broader economic confidence for other people to start investing in the economy to make it happen.

One of the most criminal things Bolger did was to talk the country down after December 1990. He clearly communicated that New Zealand was a no-hope place full of no-hopers. We hadn't worked hard enough, we hadn't done this, we hadn't done that. There was almost no hope in trying. I think that communicated itself quite widely. People got very depressed. We've got to bring some hope. We would be foolish to be promising miracles, because there aren't any. If there were, someone would have discovered them. But I think we have to promise hope and the prospect that, for the effort you put in, there'll be a reward.

I've stayed in high gear in health since I stopped being Minister of Health, and it's been a long slog. It took a tremendous amount of groundwork to get the health issue to the stage where I got the scalp of the Minister of Health. That was two years of systematically knocking over the crazy things that they were doing. In the end he went for all the wrong reasons. I still maintain they sacked the wrong guy because Birch and Bolger are as guilty as Upton.

In the months since Bill Birch has been health minister it's been my job to point out that nothing has changed. All Bill Birch will do is spend millions more of our money to try to tell us that what we don't want is good for us. That's not a change. But it's taken a lot of work to get public feeling on the matter to where it is now.

Health is swinging back towards institutions and technology with the dollar being the only thing that counts. That's totally antithetical to women's health needs. The signs are, when you look at household expenditure, that women are going without in terms of shoes and clothing. Expenditure on that is way, way down, because household budgets are having to pay out up to thirty per cent more on education costs, twenty-two per cent more on health care costs, eighteen per cent more on pharmaceuticals. So women miss out. In education the mature student is greatly disadvantaged because of differential fees. Everything is operating against women trying to pull themselves up by their bootstraps.

The government cut back the child care subsidies. Take things like the restructuring of Plunket. Plunket's not a government organization but it's restructuring to meet the government's demand for the contract—a hundred Plunket nurses down the tubes. That directly affects women. It's just one thing after another. And to see Jenny Shipley going around the country crowing as the Queen of Women's Suffrage in Centennial year, it makes me cringe.

Birch hasn't yet moved to repeal the Minimum Wage Act. The Employers' Federation probably wants that. The Round Table wants it, Treasury wouldn't object. Just let wages find their own level in the market. The minimum wage is $6.125 an hour. It hasn't changed since I adjusted it to that in 1990.

But there's no real recourse for someone who's earning $3.00 an hour. Firstly, the disempowered worker won't have a clue that they're $3.12 an hour under. Secondly, if they did have, would they be so rash as to put the only job going on the line by going to the Employment Court? Birch has made the Employment Court so legalistic you've got to employ lawyers and so on. You can't enforce it.

It's the same as with the minimum code. With the Employment Contracts Act we managed to get some minimal provisions in, but you can't enforce it because people are too terrified. In the whole of New Zealand there are seven Labour Department inspectors, and they're so busy answering the phones they actually never enforce anything.

So many of these changes primarily affect women. Employment equity, that was the first to go. The changes in housing support affect women disproportionately, because women require housing disproportionately. The Corporation was targeted to helping the neediest, and women were the neediest, in terms of single-parent families, older single women, Māori women. So that is devastating to women: the change to full market rent and inadequate subsidies.

When you're in a depression, and when the State is cutting back, the process is in danger of becoming permanent. The underclass can never find its way out; it's so preoccupied with the sheer business of survival it can't see beyond that. Another three to six years of what we're going through now will see voting participation in this country way, way down. We just won't be able to mobilize the permanently unemployed, the disempowered Pacific Island people, a lot of Māori.

You can only change it by change of government and change of policies. You build back in the supports for the low-income people so that they don't have to worry about where their next crust is coming from. They need to know that services are more accessible, that the local school is properly funded and resourced and they don't have to be terrified of taking a sick child to the doctor because they can't pay. Very basic little things. The rent has to be manageable, They have to know that their Housing Corp landlord isn't going to throw them out.

One of the objectives of the Department of Social Welfare was to enable people to participate. It wasn't just maintaining them to a certain minimum level, it was to enable them to participate in their society. When Shipley became minister she chucked that out. The last thing she wants is for them to have a voice. This is deliberate, this is political; it's ideological.

How did the Tories survive in Britain? They survived by the two-thirds/one-third society. Why write about the unemployed? Why have TV on the unemployed? Eighty-five per cent of the people are employed. You can cut off a whole swathe of the lower end. Once they give up the Tories have won, and it'll never change.

The haves tend to hear what you have to say about the have-nots and say, 'Well, what's in that for us? All Labour cares about is the no-hoper.' I get that all the time from middle-income earners. And it's true that the middle-income group is where the votes are. It's hard going when the consensus in Society breaks down and the power and initiative lies with the New Right. Where does the social democratic party go for resources? You're really cut off.

We spent three million on the election in 1987 and that was ridiculously high. I think there ought to be limits for everyone. I think you could probably fund an election for everyone for three million dollars. Just say, 'That's it, that's the limit on spending.'

I'm adamantly in support of State funding of elections because a reforming social democratic party will systematically burn off powerful interests who don't like what it's doing. I helped burn off pharmaceutical companies, tobacco companies, medics. As Minister of Conservation I alienated mining companies, marina companies, developers. I burned off employers with employment equity, arbitration.

I'll admit it, from the point of view of trying to fund the party, I was a menace. I've no doubt about that. In the countries where social democratic parties thrive they're State-funded. They allow for that imbalance of power. But in this country, you're a poor and struggling party if you don't have big corporates on side.

You could apply the principle they talk about so much but never apply, which is transparency. They use transparency in the sense that everything a government department does has to be transparent, for example, Radio New Zealand. You have to have absolute transparency about what you've used in your commercial revenue-generating statements, and what is used elsewhere. Why not apply the principle to election funding?

That would be an absolutely critical change. It would take away a lot of the power of the corporates. If you get rid of corporate donations to parties, you open up the whole political process. You open up the budget process, open up the Treasury advice.

I think the decent society has to accept that there's a social responsibility to health care, social responsibility for decent housing, social responsibility for ensuring that people from all income groups have access to a full range of educational and training opportunities, social responsibility for seeing that practices that discriminate against women in the workplace are countered.

In the last two and a half years, in all those areas, social responsibility has gone down the plughole. Responsibility is thrown back at individuals and no helping hand is given.

The present Government is on the verge of refusing to acknowledge that it has social responsibility. Responsibility is placed back on the individual to do their best for themselves and their families which, taken to the ultimate, breaks down society itself.

I don't think they have a clear concept of society. Everything is thought of in terms of individual responsibility and individuals' rights. They certainly don't see it as their responsibility to provide affirmative action measures which would help level out the playing-field for women. There is no level playing-field.

Unfortunately among Tory women there is a tendency to think that, because they made it and they didn't need help, therefore everybody else should make it the way they did. The way things have been, women don't make it in the same numbers as men, which means there's a structural problem. You need to address the structural problem, but they're not particularly interested in that.

Anne Collins

We're meant to be more caring, meant to be more co-operative, working in a consensus. There's absolutely no guarantee that women are going to work like that.

There's that awful funny feeling at the moment. Two of the most powerful ministers in this present Government are women, and they're just being so horrible to women. But the arguments about wanting more women—people just look at you now and say, 'Look at Ruth and Jenny. God!' So you've got to get good women in the House.

You have certain expectations of women. We're meant to be more caring, meant to be more co-operative, working in a consensus. There's absolutely no guarantee that women are going to work like that. I still think that if you've got two equal candidates going for selection and one's a woman, I'd still try and select the woman

One of the things that upsets me is what's happened to the Employment Equity Act. I chaired that committee and spent a huge amount of time on it. Employment equity got finally passed in July 1990, so it was very late in the piece. But I always knew that it wouldn't be around if National won.

Basically it was equal pay for work of equal value. The ability for women's groups to actually have a job evaluation and pit it against a similar job, as far as training, responsibility, and qualifications went. It was very sad to see that go. There wasn't time for it to have a trial, but then again I didn't have any illusions that it would stay with a National Government.

There have been some dreadful things taken away. Money for women's refuges. The effect that the benefit cuts have had on domestic violence and stress. The housing —when I became an MP, housing was our number one problem. I think most MPs would say that. For my first eighteen months, my electorate clinic was just clogged with people trying to get a house, and basically by the time we went out that had disappeared. A constituent with a housing problem was so rare. It was wonderful. And that's all coming back again, and it's so depressing, because you know that if Labour gets back in we'll have to start all over again. Women always suffer first in a housing crisis.

I had two main reasons for going into Parliament—one was the anti-nuclear issue and the other was for better staff-to-class ratios for junior classes. Once again the clock's just been turned backwards there. Graduates coming out of teachers' college can't get a job. There's just nothing going. All those little kids who are just coming into school to learn to read and write have got big classes again. That makes me absolutely furious, because it's not a huge amount of money but it's a huge impact on people's lives. If they don't learn to read and write in the first few years of school, they don't get off to a good start. So that's an issue that burns me up.

I wouldn't be the greatest role model for getting women into Parliament because I look at anybody going to Parliament pretty strangely these days. But they certainly do improve the place, improve the tone of the debates and the work that goes on .

I guess that what we have to do is, if a woman is keen and wants to go in, you just support them. I just started working for Annette King, on her campaign committee. So I'm supporting her, giving her my time, my friendship and working for her. And if she needs me when she's an MP again, I'll be there. And I think that's the most you can do.

Lianne Dalziel

. . . you can talk about this level playing-field but I'm not quite sure I know what that means. Well, I suppose level can mean vertical, can't it?

In some areas people will be able to protect their interests reasonably well, even under the Employment Contracts Act, but in other areas it's just gone splat. Without the compulsory new membership provisions there are a lot of extremely vulnerable people out there in the smaller worksites. It's as simple as that.

Women have traditionally worked in the round-the-clock industries, service industries, nursing. When they say the average wage, they don't look at overtime. But overtime they classify as penal rates, so loss of penal rates may in fact mean there's been an overall reduction in people's take-home pay. If the latest household survey on spending power is to be believed, that's been reduced for the first time since 1973.

And a lot of people in that middle-income bracket are really being knocked around, particularly if they've got kids at varsity under twenty-five, because they then become very dependent on their parents again, just when they think they've got rid of them.

Jenny Shipley's reality is not the reality that I confront in my electorate. I have people sitting in my office regularly who I'm seriously concerned about in terms of whether they're going to consider taking their own lives.

I'm really worried at the moment about a guy who came in to see me last weekend. It's about child support payments. The child support payments hit pretty heavily on someone who's on his own, but he's got personal commitments and they aren't taken into account. There's a set amount to pay based on your income. He has health problems too. He had an epileptic fit when he read the letter from the child support agency. I've been thinking about him all week. He's really depressed and there's nothing I can do for him. We have no power over the agency. They have to implement set figures in the Act, there are no discretions and if you don't like the decision the only thing you can do is go to the Family Court.

The Employment Contracts Act has made people extremely vulnerable. The language that goes with it, this freedom of choice, individual freedom of choice, that's the line. I've always felt that you've got to look behind the language to see what they're really saying.

Individuals only have freedom when there's choice for all. When the collectives are working, and those are your unions, your families, your societies, your communities, then individuals do have freedom of choice. But when the collectives aren't working, and I don't believe any of those collectives are working at the moment, then the only individuals with freedom of choice are those with power, position, or money. They're the only individuals who have freedom of choice at the moment. I mean you can talk about this level playing-field but I'm not quite sure I know what that means. Well, I suppose level can mean vertical, can't it?

Fran Wilde

. . . the most vulnerable politically are the women and children.

What's gone? Early childhood education is the major area. It's not just good for women, it's good for the whole society. But the women MPs pushed it. That was our policy. We got it into the mainstream of the party and it became the core of our education policy—early childhood had priority.

Initially we had to fight everybody, but we just pushed it through the system. The women were very cohesive in the party in those days. This was, I guess, between '81 and '84 when we were in Opposition, but we knew we were on the verge of being in Government. I have no doubt that early childhood education was one of our best policies in terms of long-term investment in the community—in all ways, social, economic, everything. It's been the stupidest thing the Nats have done to pull out funding in that area.

There was a whole range of other things. Pay equity was obviously one. That whole EEO area. Also some of the health initiatives. They just weren't entrenched enough. They hadn't been mainstream for long enough to be untouchable. Mind you, nothing's untouchable with this Government.

But they picked on what they perceived to be the fringe things first. Things like domestic violence. They haven't unwound that, but they've cut down the voluntary agency funding. The delivery agencies for the voluntary sector have lost their resources. The needy groups are the ones who have the least voice. And the most vulnerable politically are the women and children.

So policies that benefit women have been attacked. It always happens when social services delivery is attacked, because women are the bottom of the heap. So, whether it's by design or accident, it happens. The National Party have just said, well it's part of the cuts. All the talk about law and order and all the talk about violence is just populism. If they wanted to do something about it they'd enhance early childhood education. It's a very strong, powerful argument in that regard. They must know, but they choose to ignore it.

I don't know how you get more women into Parliament. It's no fit place for anyone if they want to maintain some sense of normality. A lot of my friends have said, 'We understand why you're getting out, but we wish you weren't.' That's not because I'm anything marvellous, it's just because I'm another person who's tried to maintain a bit of normality. But no one could say my life has been normal. It's notable that it's the women MPs who leave voluntarily. People like Anne Collins, Ann Hercus, and Marilyn Waring. How many men—apart from those who reach retirement age—have actually got out?

Margaret Austin

There's a great sadness in New Zealand . . .

The situation now is so alien to my value system that I am getting more and more angry. We have got probably one of the most authoritarian Governments that this country has ever seen. Their dismissal of people who might be able to make an input is so all-encompassing that it doesn't matter what issue it is or what aspect of things they're trying to change, everything is being steamrollered through.

The education sector is in turmoil over wages and conditions. Nobody's asking for money, but nothing can be agreed to between the parties in negotiation without the Cabinet committee sanctioning it. That's not negotiation, that's dictatorship.

These people have been very well trained by Muldoon, and they haven't forgotten anything. And if you were to ask me do they want power? Yes, they want power and they will do anything to keep it.

I'm not sure how to get young people involved in politics. I made a speech the other night to the Hornby Promotion Association, because we've had great difficulty keeping the thing activated. People like to see the functions like Christmas pageants and Daffodil Day. But we've come up against a brick wall of apathy in getting people involved enough to help those of us who want to see that things succeed. I said in the speech that public perception was all wrong because they saw it as being a business persons' association not an association for the people. If we are going to succeed we have to prise people out from behind their brick or wooden fences. It seems to me people have retreated behind their fences.

You talk to people on the doorstep and you find an enormous number of people are at sporting events with their children or in their own right. There are some things on that people just flock to. Perhaps involvement in the mere issues of the day doesn't seem to matter to them. They know they're being affected, they're hurting. They know that inside they're angry. They don't know what to do about it. So they either lock themselves away or they get involved so they can take their minds off it.

There's a great sadness in New Zealand that we have been reduced to people turning up at foodbanks. That the most successful shops are op shops. In a sense I feel a sort of personal guilt because of what you are and what you've done. And I feel this enormous frustration at this society in front of you becoming an eighty/twenty society—where eighty per cent of people are doing quite well and twenty per cent are just coping.

Judith Tizard

. . . paying the poor less and less does not seem to be making them work harder and harder.

Politics is how you distribute resources, and you can let the rich grab more, or you can say, 'No, we don't accept poverty. We won't accept denial of basic needs, such as housing, health care, and education.' It's very simple, it seems to me.

My grandparents came to New Zealand because they were rejecting a class system in Britain. We are increasingly perpetuating that class system here. I don't think it's acceptable that old people live in poverty, I don't think it's acceptable that children are brought up in poverty.

If we choose in terms of efficiency, it is more efficient to fund the providers of services than to fund the users. If you fund the users then they will have to make their economic decisions in a way that's not always going to have long-term benefits. Or you make sure that child care is available, early childhood education, good secondary schools, good universities are provided, make sure that, if people are sick, they can get the medical attention they require. We can make sure that the government builds houses that keep the market at a level that families can afford. That's a more efficient use of resources than just throwing money up into the sky and saying, 'Let's all of us just grab all we can.'

J. K. Galbraith said recently that he found it extraordinary the monetarist theory seemed to be saying if you paid the rich more then they would work harder, but if you paid the poor less they would work harder. Human beings tend to react to similar signals, and paying the poor less and less does not seem to be making them work harder and harder.

Annette King

I believe less of what I hear from politicians.

Since 1990, from the outside looking in, I've become very much like the public in many ways. I believe less of what I hear from politicians. It's a difficult role because when you're part of what's happening it's hard to see anything else. It's hard to see another point of view. I feel more cynical about politics and politicians and that's been helped by what's happened since 1990. As a party that had been in Government for a handful of times over forty years, we made mistakes.

The National Party saw the mistakes we made. You could hear what the public was saying because they were braying it back to us. To turn around and in a matter of weeks break all the promises they'd made was unforgivable. I mean, hell, if we haven't learnt something from the mistakes we made in six years in Government. If we win in November and we repeat those same mistakes, I don't believe we ever deserve to be back in Government again.

You should learn from it, surely to God. I couldn't believe that the National Party didn't learn from our mistakes. They were, within a matter of weeks, breaking all those promises to the elderly. Take a seat like Horowheneua. The electorate had a lot of elderly people who were really keen for the promises that Bolger made on superannuation. For hundreds of them, thousands of them around New Zealand, to cynically change every one of them was unbelievable.

Margaret Shields

. . . once you're out you've got time to reflect . . .

I'm still in politics of course, but it's a different kind. One of the nice things is that a lot of the experience has been extremely useful. You know, it's a toughening experience, you learn a lot. But once you're out you've got time to reflect, you've got more time to read, and you can get it all a bit more into perspective.

Katherine O'Regan

It's wrong for women to always blame men for not making the grade.

If women want to be in politics, they have to make that decision—they must know that they want to do something like this. It's important to be involved in the party, to get to be known by the people in your electorate, to attend conferences, and be a part of a policy-making group.

Learn when not to push yourself. People who are pushy get right up the nostrils of everybody. It doesn't matter if it's a man or a woman. Women have got to realize—and this is one small criticism that I do have of women—that they cannot always blame being a woman as the reason why they have not been accepted. There is a thing called personality that maybe people do not like or feel uncomfortable with. So one's got to be realistic about these things. It's wrong for women to always blame men for not making the grade.

Women will never improve themselves unless they take a really hard look at themselves and say, 'Look, is it because I'm a woman, or is it because of something I've said or done, or how I've behaved, or perhaps I've stepped on somebody's toes? Maybe I should learn from this.' We have to look at ourselves and see how as individuals and as human beings we actually perform.

Women on women are very tough as well. Even if you had a whole selection committee of women I believe you'd still have as many views. Some of them might even be harder and the reasons for that may be a sense of long-term frustration and envy that maybe these young things are doing things that I'd love to have done but couldn't do. There's something at the back of the head, I don't know what it is, that prevents them saying, 'Isn't this wonderful, these young women are getting in there. I'm going to get out there and support them.'

There are a lot of those women around. We talked about this in the lobby the other day, Gail McIntosh and myself. It's a generalization, but we decided it was the young women and the older men who are more supportive of women candidates. Young men feel threatened and older women look back perhaps in envy. So it really only leaves younger women and the older men, who stay apart, who can actually turn around and say, 'Look, it's dead right, we should have more women.'

As women politicians, I think Ruth Richardson, Jenny Shipley, and Helen Clark are probably the three who have had the most influence. And Marilyn, of course, in her time. But I think they still are seen as exceptions. A good test will be to see whether the Waipa electorate, when I choose to stand down, will select another woman candidate. It's already had two. My guess is that it probably wouldn't, which is a pity. We'll see; give them another few years and the whole attitude may change, but today it may not be so.

Marilyn's quite right that it's not just individual women that will change it, it will be women collectively over a period of time, over a period of decades. It will take that long I think for absolute total acceptance to take place.

Marilyn Waring

Parliament is not going to change in a hurry. Not unless we work out a way to remove testosterone at age twelve . . .

Anyone thinking of going in—don't compromise. Especially if you're young. You've got a lot more years to go yet, and you've got to live with all of that. And nothing is worth, as Bernadette Devlin would have put it, 'the price of your soul'.

My entire experience in Parliament—three was the maximum number of women [National] ever had. So I can't generalize to the numbers they have now. The only people who shared Caucus situations with me were Colleen Dewe and Ruth Richardson. None of us shouted. I certainly cried from time to time. But none of us shouted.

Whereas inside Caucus I have seen John Banks walking across the room with his fists raised wanting to punch somebody out—one of his own colleagues. Yeah, people screamed hell at each other. Boys were boys you know?

Parliament is not going to change in a hurry. Not unless we work out a way to remove testosterone at age twelve, it won't. That's my latest science fiction endeavour. And then women in charge of the males can apply to the government for injections so they can get it up every now and then.

For feminists—who I believe have a raging sense of humour—it's a very humourless time.

You can put women anywhere you like, but if they aren't there to transform the institution then you haven't changed anything much. I mean just getting a lot more oestrogen around a table does not change the situation if each of those women have arrived there through a socialized, patriarchal, institutional climb.

If you're a woman in politics, loads of people say, 'Oh but women don't make any difference, look at Thatcher.' My reply is always to say, 'Listen if I took one man and locked him up in an institution with 650 women he'd be a bloody strange man by the end of it.' And I sincerely mean exactly the same about taking women and putting them inside patriarchal institutions. If they then behave and conform according to the institution's rules, nothing changes. The only reason for women to be in these institutions is to transform them. If they're not transforming them, we're not making any progress. Really, if they aren't there as radicals to transform the place . . .

That doesn't mean that, with increasing numbers, the tenor of the debate doesn't change. There's no question that the main reason it's a little better is because there are more women there. Similarly the US House of Congress is going to find things on its agenda it never thought of before, with its recent influx. But a lot of those things very frequently are just going to be reformist.

If women had any gumption they would have said during this entire electoral reform process, 'Whatever the outcome we want parity—fifty per cent of the seats—you can vote for MMP, STV, FPP whatever you bloody well like. But when it comes down to it, every party must field the equal number of candidates and make sure they're equally in seats.' That's what we should have been doing.

We're really missing the boat, getting distracted. I think that happens far too frequently in the movement in this country. Getting bought off by the cheapest, smallest, next reform. Being promised the moon for the next little incremental step. Instead of saying, 'Oh fuck that. This is what we want.'

Appendices

1. New Zealand Women Members of Parliament

AUSTIN, Margaret Elizabeth

Labour   Yaldhurst   1984–

Political experience: Member of Labour Party since 1972. Elected MP for Yalhurst, 1984, at age 51 (seat formerly held by Hon. Mick Connelly (L)); member Communications and Road Safety select committees; appointed Senior Government Whip, 1987; achieved Cabinet rank, 1990: Minister of Internal Affairs, Minister of Arts and Culture, Minister of Civil Defence, Minister of Research, Science and Technology.

Other details: (b. 1933); BSc (Canterbury/London), Dip.Tchg; Head of Science, Christchurch High School; Senior Mistress, Riccarton High; Fellowship in Biology (1970)—with special interest in curriculum development and education administration; Commonwealth Trust Fellowship (1980)—to research secondary school curriculum at Institute of Education, London; Executive Secretary, first Roman Catholic Diocesan Pastoral Council; council member, Ecological Society and Royal Society of New Zealand, Canterbury Branch; president, Education Administration Society; instrumental in setting up the New Zealand Science Teachers' Association; member, Canterbury Regional Development Council, Lincoln College Council, Canterbury Medical Research Council, Canterbury Provincial Buildings Board.

BATCHELOR, Mary Dorothy

Labour   Avon   1972–87

Political experience: President of St Albans women's branch of the Labour Party; executive member, Labour Regional Council; first woman nominated to stand in a safe Labour seat. Elected MP for Avon, General Election, 1972, at age 45 (seat formerly held by Jock Mathison (L)); reselected 1983 despite challenge for candidacy. Retired August 1987, prior to commencement of selection procedure for General Election.

Other details: (b. 1927); worked as shop assistant and sewing machine demonstrator; organizer for Canterbury Clerical Workers' Union; represented Pegasus ward on Christchurch City Council from 1971, combining this role with parliamentary duties.

CLARK, Helen Elizabeth

Labour   Mt Albert   1981–

Political experience: Joined Labour Party 1970; former president, Labour Youth Council and secretary, Labour Women's Council; executive member, New Zealand Labour Party; unsuccessfully contested Piako (safe National seat) 1975. Elected MP for Mt Albert, 1981, aged 31 (seat formerly held by Hon. Warren Freer (L)); chaired Foreign Affairs and Defence select committee; Minister of Housing and Minister of Conservation (1987); Minister of Health (February, 1989); Minister of Labour (August, 1989) and Deputy Prime Minister—the first woman in New Zealand's history to hold this office; first New Zealand woman to be appointed to the Privy Council.

Other details: (b. 1951); MA(Hons)(Auckland); former Lecturer in Political Studies, University of Auckland.

COLLINS, Lowson Anne—see: FRASER

DALZIEL, Lianne

Labour   Christchurch Central   1990–

Political experience: Former member Christchurch Central LEC; executive member, Canterbury Regional Council, New Zealand Labour Party. Elected MP for Christchurch Central in General Election, 1990, at age 30 (seat formerly held by Rt. Hon. Geoffrey Palmer (L)).

Other details: (b. 1960); attended University of Canterbury, graduated in Law; admitted to Bar as barrister and solicitor, 1984; has worked as kitchenhand, cleaner in a public hospital; involved with Hotel and Hospital Workers' Union; union organizer, legal officer, and union secretary; Canterbury representative on National Council of New Zealand Council of Trade Unions from its inception.

DAVIES, Sonja Margaret Loveday

Labour   Pencarrow   1987–

Political experience: Joined Nelson branch of Labour Party in 1950s; served in various capacities: branch secretary, secretary of Nelson Labour Representation Committee, member, National Executive, member Labour Women's Advisory Committee. Elected MP for Pencarrow in General Election, 1987, at age 63 (seat formerly held by Hon. Fraser Colman (L)).

Other details: (b. 1923); Trainee nurse, shop employee, library assistant; assistant secretary/organizer, Public Service Association, Wellington regional office, 1971–73; regional representative, New Zealand Food Processing Union and Wellington Clerical Union; first woman to be elected to the executive of the Federation of Labour; vice-president of FOL, 1981–87; founder member, New Zealand Association of Child Care Centres; founder of the New Zealand Working Women's Council; co-organizer, New Zealand Working Women's Convention (1977); vice-president, New Zealand Peace Council; led New Zealand delegation to World Peace Conference (1990). Local body involvement included membership of: Nelson Hospital Board, Nelson City Council, New Zealand Municipal Electricity Committee. Awarded Order of New Zealand; Justice of the Peace; Marriage Celebrant; honorary Doctor of Laws, Victoria University, Wellington.

DEWE, Colleen Elizabeth

National   Lyttelton   1975–78

Political experience: Worked for Harry Lake during 1957 General Election campaign; held various National Party offices—treasurer, Canterbury–Westland division, Dominion councillor. Elected MP for Lyttelton, 1975 (defeating sitting Member, Tom McGuigan (L)); served on various select committees; defeated, 1978, by Ann Hercus (L).

Other details: (b. 1930; d. 1993); attended University of Canterbury; graduated ACA; after 1978 defeat, appointed to Commerce Commission; chaired Advisory Committee on women.

DREAVER, Mary Manson MBE

Labour   Waitemata   1941–43

Political experience: Joined Women's International Political League (later Auckland Women's Branch of Labour Party), 1922; many years member of executive of Auckland Labour Party; first served on Auckland City Council, 1938–44; first woman appointed to Transport Board; served on Auckland Hospital Board, 1933–44. Elected MP for Waitemata, 1941, aged 54 (in By-election after incumbent, William Lyon (L) was killed on active service); defeated in General Election, 1943; appointed to Legislative Council, 1946; returned to local body politics after defeat. Served at various times on Auckland City Council, Auckland Metropolitan Drainage Board, Auckland Electric Power Board, Auckland Hospital Board.

Other details: (b. 1887; d. 1961); educated at University of Auckland; gained LLCM from London College of Music; taught drama, public speaking, music, hosted radio programmes directed at women; served as vice-president of New Zealand Fellowship of Artists; member of Theosophist Society—first woman ordained as minister in the National Spiritualist Church; Justice of the Peace; awarded MBE for public service, 1946.

Catherine Stewart, MP for Wellington West, 1938–43. Alexander Turnbull Library ref. no. 154218½

At Port Waikato Children's Health Camp, 1930s. The Camp's founders with Hilda (later Dame Hilda) Ross, MP for Hamilton, 1945–59; Minister without portfolio, 1949–57; Minister of Social Security, 1957. Waikato Museum of Art and History, ref. 10619

Mary Dreaver MBE, MP for Waitemata, 1941–43. From a group portrait of the Auckland City Council, 1938–41. Auckland Public Library, A12585

Lady William Polson (formerly Mary Grigg, MP for Mid-Canterbury, 1942–43) at her husband's investiture, April 1952. Alexander Turnbull Library

FLETCHER, Christine Elizabeth

National   Eden   1990–

Political experience: Member of Young Nationals; branch chairperson, Eden Nationals; representative on Divisional Women's Committe. Elected MP for Eden, 1990, at age 35 (defeating sitting Member Richard Northey (L)).

Other details: (b. 1955); educated at St Cuthberts College, Auckland and University of Auckland; held administrative and managerial positions in family firm, Lees Industries; involved in VSA; trustee, Substance Abuse Education Trust; worker for Foundation for Alcohol and Drug Education (FADE); foundation member, Red Cross Auxilliary.

FRASER (Collins), Lowson Anne

Labour   East Cape   1984–90

Political experience: Joined Labour Party, 1982—secretary, Whakatane Branch. Elected MP for East Cape, 1984, aged 32 (replacing retiring Member, Hon. Duncan McIntyre (N)); served on various select committees including Education and Science; decided not to stand in 1990 General Election and retired from Parliament.

Other details: (b. 1952); BEd. (Massey); worked as salaries clerk and teacher; founder member Whakatane Nuclear Weapons-free Zone Group, 1982; reverted to maiden name, Anne Collins, July 1989; married Labour front-bencher, Dr Michael Cullen, December 1989.

GRIGG, Mary Victoria Cracroft MBE

National   Mid-Canterbury   1942–43

Political experience: Attended to electorate duties after her husband, Arthur Grigg (National MP for Mid-Canterbury, 1938–41) joined Army; served on National Party Dominion Executive; entered Parliament aged 45 at By-election, 1942, after husband killed on active service; did not seek reselection at General Election of 1943; first National Party woman to be nominated, selected, and elected after the Party's formation in 1936; remained active in the National Party after her retirement; supported Dame Hilda Ross.

Other details: (b. 1897; d. 1971); involved in VAD nursing service in England during World War I; president, Ashburton Plunket Society; member, Ashburton Hospital Board; second marriage to Hon. William Polson (MP for Stratford, 1928–46).

HASLER, Marie Bernarde

National   Titirangi   1990–

Political experience: Treasurer, New Lynn electorate committee of National Party; executive member, Titirangi branch of National Party. Elected MP for Titirangi, 1990, aged 45 (defeating sitting Member, Ralph Maxwell (L)).
Other details: (b. 1945); attended University of Auckland; currently studying towards MBA; formerly a retail manager, owning own business, 1982–87; has worked in public relations, advertising, public service.

HERCUS, Dame Margaret Ann

Labour   Lyttelton   1978–87

Political experience: Joined Labour Party in her late twenties. Elected MP for Lyttelton, 1978, aged 36 (defeating Colleen Dewe (N))—the first campaign in New Zealand history in which all candidates were women; Opposition spokesperson on Consumer Affairs, Health, Social Welfare, Women's Affairs, and associate spokesperson for Trade and Industry; served six years on Public Expenditure Committee; candidate, in 1983, for Deputy Leadership of Labour Party—came third, behind Geoffrey Palmer and Mike Moore; from 1984, Minister of Social Welfare and Minister of Police—the first woman in the world to hold this portfolio; Minister responsible for setting up Ministry of Women's Affairs; retired from Parliament at General Election, 1987.
Other details: (b. 1942); BA (Auckland/Victoria); law degree from Univerity of Canterbury involvement with Plunket Society; served on management committees of Hutt/Wairarapa and Canterbury Playcentre Associations; president, Christchurch branch of the Society for Research on Women; member, Christchurch district committee of the Consumers' Institute; appointed to Price Tribunal and Trade Practices Commision, 1973; deputy chairperson, Commerce Commission, 1975; after retirement took up position as New Zealand's permanent representative to the United Nations; currently an international consultant; created DBE, 1988.

HOWARD, Mabel Bowden

Labour   Christchurch East   1943–46
                                Sydenham   1946–69

Political experience: Daughter of E. J. Howard (Labour MP for Christchurch South, 1919–39); overlooked as a candidate for her father's seat after his death in 1939. Elected MP for Christchurch East (later renamed Sydenham), 1943 (in By-election after the death of the incumbent, H. T.

Armstrong (L)), aged 49; first woman in New Zealand and the Commonwealth to be appointed to Cabinet; Minister of Health, 1947–49; Minister of Social Security and Minister in Charge of the Welfare of Women and Children, 1957–60; retired because of ill-health.
Other details: (b. 1894; d. 1972); secretary, Canterbury Labourers' Union; first woman to be appointed National Secretary of New Zealand Federated Labourers' Union.

JELICICH, Dorothy Catherine

Labour   Hamilton West   1972–75
Political experience: Joined Papatoetoe women's branch of Labour Party, 1957; contested Hauraki for Labour in 1969, significantly reducing National's majority. Elected MP for Hamilton West, 1972, aged 44; first woman in New Zealand's parliamentary history to open the Address in Reply debate; first woman to lead an all-women delegation to a United Nations Population Conference, 1974; defeated in 1975 election by Michael Minogue (N); stood for Hamilton West in 1978 election but was defeated.
Other details: (b. 1928); early experience as retailer, restaurant owner, Shop Assistants' Union organizer, and dairy farmer; Manukau City councillor since 1981.

KEALL, Judith Mary (Judy)

Labour   Glenfield   1984–90
Political experience: Elected MP for Glenfield, 1984, aged 41; served on various select committees; chairperson, Social Services select committee; Junior Government Whip from March 1990. Defeated in General Election, 1990.
Other details: (b.1942); MA(Hons) (Auckland), Dip. Tchg; factory, hospital, and retail worker while at university; secondary school teacher before entering Parliament; Auckland Regional Authority candidate, 1983; patron, North Shore Solo Parents' Club.

KING, Annette Faye

Labour   Horowhenua   1984–90
Political experience: Joined Labour Party, Hamilton, 1972; branch and LEC delegate and a member of the Wellington LEC. Elected MP for Horowhenua, 1984, aged 37 (defeated sitting Member, Geoff Thompson (N); achieved Cabinet rank, August 1989—Minister of Employment, Minister of Immigration, Minister of Youth Affairs, and special role as Minister assisting

the Prime Minister to liaise between Cabinet and Caucus; formerly Parliamentary Under-Secretary to Ministers of Employment, Youth Affairs, Tourism, and Social Welfare; standing as Labour candidate for Miramar in 1993 General Election.
Other details: (b. 1947); BA (Waikato); trained as a school dental nurse; dental tutor; National Vice-President, New Zealand State Dental Nurses' Institute; PSA delegate; after losing her seat, appointed Chief Executive Officer, Palmerston North Enterprise Board.

KIRK, Jennifer Norah (Jenny)

Labour   Birkenhead   1987–90
Political experience: Joined Glenfield Labour Party, 1983; electorate office assistant to Judy Keall, 1984–85; electorate secretary and executive member, Glenfield and Birkenhead LECs; founding member, North Shore Labour Women's Collective. Elected MP for Birkenhead, 1987, aged 43 (seat formerly held by Hon. Jim McLay (N)); member of various select committees, including Justice and Law Reform, Social Services. Defeated in General Election, 1990.
Other details: (b. 1945); attended business college; secretarial work, hotel/motel management; reporter for *North Shore Times Advertiser* and journalist on business house magazines; member, National Organisation for Women; since defeat has returned to journalism as editor of *Communicate*, magazine of the National Foundation for the Deaf.

McCOMBS, Elizabeth Reid

Labour   Lyttelton   1933–35
Political experience: Early involvement with the Fabian Society; executive member, Canterbury Progressive Liberal Association; member, Social Democratic Party; founder member, New Zealand Labour Party, 1916; unsuccesfully contested Kaiapoi for Labour, 1928, and Christchurch North, 1931. Elected MP for Lyttelton in By-election, September 1933, aged 60 (after the death of her husband, James McCombs, who had held Lyttelton since 1913); first woman to be elected to New Zealand Parliament; died in office, 7 June 1935. Succeeded by her son, Terence.
Other details: (b. 1873; d. 1935); active in local body politics; served on Christchurch City Council, chaired Electricity Committee; member, Tramways Board, North Canterbury Hospital Board; ardent prohibitionist— president, Canterbury section and Dominion treasurer, Women's Christian Temperance Union; secretary, Canterbury Children's Aid Society.

McINTOSH, Gail Helen

National   Lyttelton   1990–
Political experience: Treasurer, Lyttelton branch, National Party, 1989–90; served on National Party Divisional Policy and Women's committees. Elected MP for Lyttelton, 1990, aged 35 (defeated sitting Member, Peter Simpson (L)); member, Finance and Expenditure select committee.
Other details: (b. 1955); attended Victoria University and University of Canterbury; BCom., ACA; worked for three years as taxi driver in Wellington; worked in accounting in Melbourne and London; employed in accounting practice in Christchurch, 1987–90; member, Heathcote Community Board, National Council of Women, Soroptimists' International.

McLAUCHLAN, Marilyn Joy

National   Western Hutt   1990–
Political experience: Involved with National Party since 1980; unsuccesfully contested Eastern Hutt for National, 1984; former parliamentary secretary to John Banks and George Gair; parliamentary executive assistant to Ruth Richardson and Don McKinnon prior to being elected to Parliament. Elected MP for Western Hutt, 1990, aged 42 (defeating sitting Member, John Terris (L)).
Other details: (b. 1948); attended Massey University, Christchurch Teachers' College, University of Otago; diploma in Physical Education; former teacher, polytechnic tutor, and research officer; director of family company; member, Pinehaven Progressive Association, 1982–84; councillor, Heretaunga Pinehaven District County Council, 1987–89; member, Lower Hutt Chamber of Commerce; District Commissioner, Girl Guides, 1984–89; supporter of Maruia Society, Wellington Rape Crisis Centre, Women Against Pornography.

McMILLAN, Ethel Emma QSO

Labour   North Dunedin   1953–63
                           Dunedin North   1963–75
Political experience: Husband, David Gervan McMillan (former MP for Dunedin West, Cabinet Minister in Fraser Ministry, 1940–41). Elected MP for North Dunedin, December 1953 (in By-election after death of Labour incumbent, Robert Walls). Elected MP for Dunedin North in General Election, 1963; retired at General Election, 1975.
Other details: (b. 1904; d. 1987); MA(Hons) (Otago); Assistant Lecturer in History, University of Otago; history mistress, Nelson Girls' College; vice-

president, Otago Boys' High School Parents' Association; governor on Otago High Schools Board for 14 years; member, executive of Otago TB Association for seven years; member, Otago Hospital Board for 16 years; member of executive, New Zealand Library Association and Dunedin Public Library; member, Otago Museum Trust Board; trustee, Dunedin Savings Bank; Dunedin City Councillor; QSO, 1976.

MOIR, Margaret

National   West Coast   1990–

Political experience: Member, National Party since 1978; chairperson, Franz Josef branch of National Party, 1978–79; stood for candidate selection on two occasions prior to 1990. Elected MP for West Coast, 1990, aged 49 (defeating sitting Member, Hon. Sir Kerry Burke (L)).

Other details: (b. 1941); co-owner, with husband, of Hokitika motorcycle shop, 1981–92; councillor, Westland County Council and Westland District Council, 1980–90; chairperson, West Coast United Council, 1986–89; chairperson, West Coast Regional Council, 1989–90; member, West Coast Regional Development Council, 1984–89; co-opted member, West Coast Business Development Board, 1989–90; member, Westland Soroptimists International.

O'REGAN, Katherine Victoria

National   Waipa   1984–

Political experience: Member, National Party, Raglan electorate, 1975–76; branch chairperson, 1976–84; deputy electorate chairperson, 1983–84, and Waikato Division Women's secretary; personal assistant to MP Marilyn Waring, 1975–84. Elected MP for Waipa, 1984 (on retirement of Marilyn Waring); Opposition spokesperson on Women's Affairs and family issues, Consumer Affairs, and Statistics; introduced private member's bill seeking recognition for children with specific learning disabilities; Minister outside Cabinet in Bolger administration—Minister of Consumer Affairs, Associate Minister of Women's Affairs, Associate Minister of Health.

Other details: (b. 1946); trained as a nurse at Waikato Hospital; has worked as a pharmacy assistant; first woman member, Waipa County Council, 1977–84; member, Waipa Health and Social Welfare Co-ordinating Committee; deputy chairperson, Hamilton Airport Authority; member, Noxious Weeds and Pest Destruction Committee; president, Hamilton Plunket Society; president, Hamilton Speech Therapy Parents' Association; member, standing committee SPELD; board member, National Society for Alcohol and Drug Addiction; member, Real Estate Agents Licensing Board; Justice of the Peace.

*Rona Stevenson MBE,
MP for Taupō, 1963–72.*
Taupo Times/Taupo
Women's Club

*Esme Tombleson QSO, MP for Gisborne, 1960–72, with an unidentified supporter,
election night, 1963.* H. B. Williams Memorial Library, Gisborne

Iriaka Matiu Rātana OBE, MP for Western Māori, 1949–69, with Manurewa MP, Phil Amos, April 1969. Christchurch Star

Ethel McMillan QSO, MP for Dunedin North/North Dunedin, 1953–75, during the 1972 election campaign. Christchurch Star

RATANA, Iriaka Matiu OBE

Labour   Western Māori   1949–69
Political experience: Elected MP for Western Māori, 1949, aged 44 (in By-election after the death of her husband, Matiu Rātana); selected after threatening to stand as an independent candidate; first Māori woman to be elected to Parliament. Retired at General Election, 1969.
Other details: (b. 1905; d. 1981); descendant of Tuwharetoa and Whanganui; daughter-in-law of Tahupotiki Wiremu Rātana; farmed with her husband at Whangaehu; strong supporter of Māori Women's Welfare League and the Māori Council; OBE, 1971.

RICHARDSON, Ruth Margaret

National   Selwyn   1981–
Political experience: Joined Young Nationals, 1968; stood unsuccessfully against Hon. W. E. Rowling (L) in Tasman, 1978; served on National Party's Agricultural Policy Committee, 1979; National Party Wellington Divisional Councillor, 1979; chaired National Party ginger group, POL-LINK. Elected MP for Selwyn, 1981, aged 30 (seat previously held by Hon. Colin McLachlan (N)); Opposition spokesperson on Education, Youth Issues, Finance; Minister of Finance in Bolger Ministry, 1990– ; first New Zealand woman to be appointed to this position.
Other details: (b. 1950); LLB (Canterbury); a farmer in her own right from 1972; legal advisor to Law Reform Division, Justice Department, 1972–75; legal advisor to Federated Farmers, 1975–81; involved in the Prime Minister's Committee on Women, steering committee, 1975–76; member, National Advisory Council on Employment of Women, 1976; member, Committee on Women, 1977; founder member, Women's Electoral Lobby.

ROSS, Dame Grace Hilda Cuthberta

National   Hamilton   1945–59
Political experience: Elected MP for Hamilton, 1945, aged 61 (By-election following the death of Frank Findlay (N)); first National Party woman to be appointed a minister; Minister without portfolio, 1949–57; Minister of Social Security, 1957 (Holyoake Ministry); first woman to act as Speaker of the House, during temporary absence of Sir Matthew Oram; died in office, 6 March 1959.
Other details: (b. 1883; d. 1959): music teacher; founder, Hamilton Choral Society; active in Hamilton Operatic Society and Orchestral Society; supporter and secretary, Waikato Children's Health Camp; member, Waikato Hospital Board, Waikato Borough Council; Deputy Mayor; president,

Women's Patriotic Committee; founded Women's Auxiliary Volunteer Corps; DBE, 1956.

SHIELDS, Margaret Kerslake

Labour   Kapiti   1981–90

Political experience: Joined Labour Party, 1969—served on the New Zealand Executive, policy council, and Labour Women's Council; stood unsuccesfully in Karori against Hugh Templeton (N), 1975; contested Kapiti against Barry Brill (N), 1978—elected on the night, but lost on an electoral recount. Elected MP for Kapiti, 1981, aged 39; achieved Cabinet ranking in the Lange Ministry; first Minister of Consumer Affairs (1984) and first Minister for Senior Citizens (1990); Minister of Customs and Associate Minister of Housing; Minister of Women's Affairs after resignation of Ann Hercus, 1987; also Minister of Statistics, Associate Minister of Education, Minister in Charge of the National Library. Defeated in General Election, 1990.

Other details: (b. 1941); BA (Victoria); worked as researcher for Consumers' Institue and Department of Statistics; co-founded Society for Research on Women; co-convenor Second United Women's Convention, 1975; delegate to United Nations International Women's Year Conference, Mexico, 1975; member, Wellington Hospital Board, 1977–80; member, Radio New Zealand Programme Committee, Wellington region; currently heading United Nations International Research and Training Institute for Advancement of Women, based in Santo Domingo.

SHIPLEY, Jennifer Mary (Jenny)

National   Ashburton   1987–

Political experience: Joined National Party, 1975; party responsibilities at branch, electorate, and divisional levels; served on Ruth Richardson's campaign committee, 1984; Selwyn Young Nationals' liaison officer, 1985; Policy Chairperson, Canterbury–Westland, 1985; divisional councillor, 1985. Elected MP for Ashburton, 1987, aged 35 (seat previously held by Hon. Rob Talbot (N), who retired); appointed to Cabinet in Bolger Ministry, 1990, after only one term in the House—Minister of Social Welfare, Minister of Women's Affairs.

Other details: (b. 1952); attended Christchurch Teachers' College and Lincoln College; primary school teacher; farmer in partnership with her husband; Malvern County Councillor, 1983–87; member, Aged People's Welfare Committee, 1983; member, Malvern Community Arts Council; served on local Plunket executive, 1979–84; president of Playcentre, 1980–82; member, Federated Farmers.

STEVENSON, Rona Miriel MBE

National   Taupō   1963–72

Political experience: Involved with National Party at branch level in Rotorua. Elected MP for the new seat of Taupō, 1963, aged 52. Retired at General Election 1972.

Other details: (b. 1911); typist; member, Board of Directors, YWCA, 1936–40; member, boards of management, Knox Church, Lower Hutt (1942–56), St Andrews, Rotorua (1954–64); long-time involvement with Women's Division of Federated Farmers at branch, provincial, and national level (1937–63)—Dominion Treasurer, 1956–63; represented New Zealand at the Helsinki Seminar on the Civil and Political Education of Women; MBE, 1976.

STEWART, Catherine Campbell Sword

Labour   Wellington West   1938–43

Political experience: Joined Socialist Party 1922; then active in Labour Party; co-founder of Elizabeth McCombs Club; first president, Melrose–Houghton Bay branch of Labour Party. Elected MP for the new seat of Wellington West, 1938, aged 57; first woman in New Zealand to be elected in a General Election. Defeated in General Election, 1943.

Other details: (b. 1881; d. 1957); Scots weaver, social worker, and former member, Glasgow Women's Collective Guild.

TENNET, Patricia Elizabeth

Labour   Island Bay   1987–

Political experience: Member, Labour Party National Executive; chairperson, Labour Women's Council; chairperson, Wellington Labour Council. Elected as MP for Island Bay, 1987 (seat previously held by Frank O'Flynn (L) who retired); served on Labour, State-Owned Enterprises select committees; secretary of Caucus; Junior Opposition Whip, 1990.

Other details: BA(Hons)(Massey/Victoria); secretary, Central Clerical Workers' Union; factory inspector, Department of Labour; researcher, Arbitration Court; member, Wellington Polytechnic Council; chairperson, Wellington Harbour Conference.

TIRIKATENE-SULLIVAN, Tini Whetu Marama

Labour   Southern Māori   1967–

Political experience: Member of Labour Party from early 1950s; member, Labour Party Māori Policy Committee; acted as confidential secretary to her father, Sir Eruera Tirikatene (Labour Member for Southern Māori, 1932–67). Elected MP for Southern Māori, 1967, aged 35 (By-election following the death of her father); appointed to Cabinet in the Kirk/Rowling Ministry, 1972–75—Minister of Tourism, Associate Minister of Social Welfare, Minister for the Environment; first Māori woman to attain Cabinet rank. *Other details:* (b.1932); stenographer, Air Department; secretary on Internal Affairs Royal Tour staff, 1953–54; secretary to Christchurch District Manager, Broadcasting Department; social worker with various government agencies—Child Welfare, Social Welfare, Māori Affairs; attended Victoria University from 1960—Diploma of Social Sciences, BA in Political Science; studied for doctorate at Australian National University, Canberra.

TIZARD, Judith

Labour   Panmure   1990–

Political experience: Researcher, Labour Opposition Research Unit; former electorate secretary, Panmure; vice-president, Labour Party Auckland Regional Council,1978–89; member, Youth Advisory Council, Labour Women's Council; unsuccessful Labour candidate in Remuera, 1981, 1987. Elected MP for Panmure, 1990, (succeeded her father, Hon. Bob Tizard (L) who retired).

Other details: (b. 1956); BA (Auckland); member, Auckland Regional Council; trustee, Friends of the Botanic Gardens; member, Ethics Committee, New Zealand Family Planning Association; board member, YWCA, 1982–85.

TOMBLESON, Esme Irene QSO

National   Gisborne   1960–72

Political experience: Elected MP for Gisborne, 1960, aged 43 (defeated sitting Member, Reginald Keeling (L)); chairperson, Māori Affairs Committee and Island Affairs Committee. Defeated in General Election, 1972.

Other details: (b. 1917); early experience in theatre and the arts; member, Imperial Society of Teachers of Dancing; associate of Australian Examination Music Board; member, Fuller's English Grand Opera Company; member, Monte Carlo Ballet Company, 1939; served with Women's Auxiliary Signalling Corps, Sydney; secretary, Manpower Advisory Board, New South Wales, 1943–47; section head, Commonwealth Employment Service, Sydney, 1947–50; QSO, 1977.

WARING, Marilyn Joy

National   Raglan   1975–78
                                Waipa   1978–84

Political experience: Researcher, National Party Research Unit. Elected MP

for Raglan (later renamed Waipa), 1975, aged 23 (seat previously held by Hon. Douglas Carter (N) who retired); youngest ever woman MP; chairperson Public Expenditure Committee (Muldoon Ministry, 1978); resigned from Caucus, 1984, prompting 'snap' election.
Other details: (b. 1952); BA(Hons)(Victoria); since resignation from Parliament has spent time developing goat farm, writing, travelling, and lecturing.

WILDE, Frances Helen (Fran)

Labour   Wellington Central   1981–92
Political experience: Joined Labour Party, 1972; electorate chairperson and member, Wellington Regional Council; editor, *New Nation*. Elected MP for Wellington Central, 1981 (defeating Ken Comber (N)); appointed Junior Whip, 1984—first woman to hold this post in the New Zealand Parliament; during 1984–87 term introduced two private member's bills—Homosexual Law Reform Bill and Adult Adoption Information Bill; Associate Minister of Foreign Affairs, Conservation, and Housing, 1987; later achieved full Cabinet rank—Minister of Disarmament and Arms Control, Minister of Tourism; Associate Minister of External Relations and Trade; lost seat on election night, 1990 but regained it after counting of special votes; retired 1992, to become Mayor of Wellington.
Other details: (b. 1948); BA (Victoria); Diploma in Journalism, Wellington Polytechnic; journalist with Radio New Zealand, print media, trade unions.

2. Women in the House—
From the 24th to the 43rd Parliament

24th Parliament 1931–35 (Coalition Government)

Elizabeth Reid McCombs (L)—By-election, 1933; died in office, 7 June 1935

25th Parliament 1935–38 (First Labour Government)

26th Parliament 1938–43 (First Labour Government)

Mary Manson Dreaver (L)—By-election, July 1941
Mary Victoria Cracroft Grigg (N)—By-election, January 1942
Mabel Bowden Howard (L)—By-election, February 1943
Catherine Campbell Sword Stewart (L)

27th Parliament 1943–46 (First Labour Government)

Mabel Bowden Howard (L)
Grace Hilda Cuthberta Ross (N)—By-election, May 1945

28th Parliament 1946–49 (First Labour Government)

Grace Hilda Cuthberta Ross (N)
Mabel Bowden Howard (L)
Iriaka Matiu Rātana (L)—By-election

29th Parliament 1949–51 (First National Government)

Grace Hilda Cuthberta Ross (N)
Mabel Bowden Howard (L)
Iriaka Matiu Rātana (L)

30th Parliament 1951–54 (First National Government)

Grace Hilda Cuthberta Ross (N)
Mabel Bowden Howard (L)

Ethel Emma McMillan (L)—By-election, December, 1953
Iriaka Matiu Rātana (L)

31st Parliament   1954–57   (First National Government)

Grace Hilda Cuthberta Ross (N)
Mabel Bowden Howard (L)
Ethel Emma McMillan (L)
Iriaka Matiu Rātana (L)

32nd Parliament 1957–60   (Second Labour Government)

Grace Hilda Cuthberta Ross (N)—died in office, 6 March 1959
Mabel Bowden Howard (L)
Ethel Emma McMillan (L)
Iriaka Matiu Rātana (L)

33rd Parliament 1960–63   (Second National Government)

Mabel Bowden Howard (L)
Ethel Emma McMillan (L)
Iriaka Matiu Rātana (L)
Esme Irene Tombleson (N)

34th Parliament 1963–66   (Second National Government)

Mabel Bowden Howard (L)
Ethel Emma McMillan (L)
Iriaka Matiu Rātana (L)
Rona Miriel Stevenson (N)
Esme Irene Tombleson (N)

35th Parliament 1966–69   (Second National Government)

Mabel Bowden Howard (L)
Ethel Emma McMillan (L)
Iriaka Matiu Rātana (L)
Rona Miriel Stevenson (N)
Tini Whetu Marama Tirikatene-Sullivan (L)—By-election, March 1967
Esme Irene Tombleson (N)

36th Parliament   1969–72   (Second National Government)

Ethel Emma McMillan (L)
Rona Miriel Stevenson (N)
Tini Whetu Marama Tirikatene-Sullivan (L)
Esme Irene Tombleson (N)

37th Parliament   1972–75   (Third Labour Government)

Mary Dorothy Batchelor (L)
Dorothy Catherine Jelicich (L)
Ethel Emma McMillan (L)
Tini Whetu Marama Tirikatene-Sullivan (L)

38th Parliament   1975–78   (Third National Government)

Mary Dorothy Batchelor (L)
Colleen Elizabeth Dewe (N)
Tini Whetu Marama Tirikatene-Sullivan (L)
Marilyn Joy Waring (N)

39th Parliament   1978–81   (Third National Government)

Mary Dorothy Batchelor (L)
Margaret Ann Hercus (L)
Tini Whetu Marama Tirikatene-Sullivan (L)
Marilyn Joy Waring (N)

40th Parliament   1981–84   (Third National Government)

Mary Dorothy Batchelor (L)
Helen Elizabeth Clark (L)
Margaret Ann Hercus (L)
Ruth Margaret Richardson (N)
Margaret Kerslake Shields (L)
Tini Whetu Marama Tirikatene-Sullivan (L)
Marilyn Joy Waring (N)
Frances Helen Wilde (L)

41st Parliament   1984–87   (Fourth Labour Government)

Margaret Elizabeth Austin (L)
Mary Dorothy Batchelor (L)
Helen Elizabeth Clark (L)
Lowson Anne Fraser (Collins) (L)
Margaret Ann Hercus (L)
Judith Mary Keall (L)
Annette Faye King (L)
Katherine Victoria O'Regan (N)
Ruth Margaret Richardson (N)
Margaret Kerslake Shields (L)
Tini Whetu Marama Tirikatene-Sullivan (L)
Frances Helen Wilde (L)

42nd Parliament   1987–90   (Fourth Labour Government)

Margaret Elizabeth Austin (L)
Helen Elizabeth Clark (L)
Sonja Margaret Loveday Davies (L)
Lowson Anne Fraser (Collins) (L)
Judith Mary Keall (L)
Annette Faye King (L)
Jennifer Norah Kirk (L)
Katherine Victoria O'Regan (N)
Ruth Margaret Richardson (N)
Margaret Kerslake Shields (L)
Jennifer Mary Shipley (N)
Patricia Elizabeth Tennet (L)
Tini Whetu Marama Tirikatene-Sullivan (L)
Frances Helen Wilde (L)

43rd Parliament   1990–93   (Fourth National Government)

Margaret Elizabeth Austin (L)
Helen Elizabeth Clark (L)
Lianne Dalziel (L)
Sonja Margaret Loveday Davies (L)
Christine Elizabeth Fletcher (N)
Marie Bernarde Hasler (N)
Gail Helen McIntosh (N)
Marilyn Joy McLauchlan (N)

Margaret Moir (N)
Katherine Victoria O'Regan (N)
Ruth Margaret Richardson (N)
Jennifer Mary Shipley (N)
Patricia Elizabeth Tennet (L)
Tini Whetu Marama Tirikatene-Sullivan (L)
Judith Tizard (L)
Frances Helen Wilde (L)—retired 1992